Biography Today

Profiles of People of Interest to Young Readers

Artists Series

Vol. 1
1996

Laurie Lanzen Harris
Executive Editor

Cherie D. Abbey
Associate Editor

Omnigraphics, Inc.

Penobscot Building
Detroit, MI 48226

Laurie Lanzen Harris, *Executive Editor*
Cherie D. Abbey, *Associate Editor*
Barry Puckett, *Research Associate*

Omnigraphics, Inc.

* * *

Matt Barbour, *Production Manager*
Laurie Lanzen Harris, *Vice President, Editorial Director*
Peter E. Ruffner, *Vice President, Administration*
James A. Sellgren, *Vice President, Operations and Finance*
Jane Steele, *Vice President, Research*

* * *

Frederick G. Ruffner, Jr., Publisher

Contents

3

Preface

Welcome to the first volume of the new **Biography Today Artists Series**. We are publishing this new series in response to the growing number of suggestions from our readers, who want more coverage of more people in *Biography Today*. This is one of five new volumes, covering **Authors, Artists, Scientists and Inventors, Sports Figures, and World Leaders,** that will be appearing in 1996 as part of the Subject Series of the *Biography Today Library*. Each of these hardcover volumes will be 200 pages in length and will cover approximately 20 individuals of interest to readers aged 9 and above. The length and format of the entries will be like those found in the regular issues of *Biography Today*, but there will be **no** duplication between the regular series and the special subject volumes.

The Plan of the Work

As with the regular issues of *Biography Today*, this special subject volume on **Artists** was especially created to appeal to young readers in a format they can enjoy reading and readily understand. Each volume contains alphabetically arranged sketches. Each entry provides at least one picture of the individual profiled, and bold-faced rubrics lead the reader to information on birth, youth, early memories, education, first jobs, marriage and family, career highlights, memorable experiences, major influences, and honors and awards. Each of the entries ends with a list of easily accessible sources designed to lead the student to further reading on the individual and a current address. Obituary entries are also included, written to provide a perspective on the individual's entire career. Obituaries are clearly marked in both the table of contents and at the beginning of the entry.

Biographies are prepared by Omni editors after extensive research, utilizing the most current materials available. Those sources that are generally available to students appear in the list of further reading at the end of the sketch.

Indexes

To provide easy access to entries, each issue of the regular *Biography Today* series and each volume of the Subject Series contains a Name Index, General Index covering occupations, organizations, and ethnic and minority origins, Places of Birth Index, and Birthday Index. These indexes cumulate with each succeeding volume or issue. Each of the volumes in the Subject Series will be indexed as part of these cumulative indexes, so that readers can locate information on all individuals covered in either the regular or the special volumes.

Our Advisors

This new member of the *Biography Today Library* of publications was reviewed by an Advisory Board comprised of librarians, children's literature specialists, and reading instructors so that we could make sure that the concept of this publication — to provide a readable and accessible biographical magazine for young readers — was on target. They evaluated the title as it developed, and their suggestions have proved invaluable. Any errors, however, are ours alone. We'd like to list the Advisory Board members, and to thank them for their efforts.

Renee Schwartz	School Board of Broward County Fort Lauderdale, FL
Lee Sprince	Broward West Regional Library Fort Lauderdale, FL
Susan Stewart	Birney Middle School Reading Laboratory, Retired Southfield, MI
Ethel Stoloff	Librarian, Birney Middle School, Retired Southfield, MI

Our Advisory Board stressed to us that we should not shy away from controversial or unconventional people in our profiles, and we have tried to follow their advice. The Advisory Board also mentioned that the sketches might be useful in reluctant reader and adult literacy programs, and we would value any comments librarians might have about the suitability of our magazine for those purposes.

Your Comments Are Welcome

Our goal is to be accurate and up-to-date, to give young readers information they can learn from and enjoy. Now we want to know what you think. Take a look at this issue of **Biography Today Artists Series**, on approval. Write or call me with your comments. We want to provide an excellent source of biographical information for young people. Let us know how you think we're doing.

And here's a special incentive: review our list of people to appear in upcoming issues. Use the bind-in card to list other people you want to see in *Biography Today*. If we include someone you suggest, your library wins a free issue, with our thanks. Please see the bind-in card for details.

Laurie Harris
Executive Editor, *Biography Today*

OBITUARY

Ansel Adams   1902–1984
American Photographer and
Environmentalist
Creator of Stunning Photographs of the
American West

BIRTH

Ansel Easton Adams was born on February 20, 1902, in San
Francisco, California. He was the only child of Olive (Bray)
Adams and Charles Hitchcock Adams, who had numerous
business interests, including a chemicals plant and an insurance agency.

YOUTH

Charles Adams came from a wealthy family who had earned their money in the lumber trade. Adams could afford to give his family just about anything, and he chose to give them a nice place to live. He built his family a beautiful house beside the Pacific Ocean in Northern California. Every morning, Ansel could see from his bedroom window one of the most majestic sights in the United States — San Francisco Bay. His boyhood playgrounds were the sand dunes of the Pacific shoreline, where he gathered shells and insects for his collections and began his lifelong love of nature. There was one drawback to this beautiful location, though: earthquakes. During the San Francisco earthquake of 1906, Ansel fell down and bashed his nose, leaving it permanently bent.

EDUCATION

Restless at the area public schools he attended, Ansel quit after the eighth grade and studied at home with his father and private tutors. Ansel taught himself to play the piano, and before long was taking lessons from an elderly German professor who taught him the works of the German baroque composer Johann Sebastian Bach and the virtues of technical excellence. "He turned me from a Sloppy Joe into a good technician," Adams said of his piano teacher. "If it hadn't been for that, I don't know what would have taken its place." He became dedicated to his music and aspired to become a classical pianist.

CHOOSING A CAREER

Ansel Adam's whole life changed when he was 14. His parents took him on a vacation to California's beautiful Yosemite National Park, where it was love at first sight. He was enchanted with Yosemite's huge, dramatic mountains and vast forests. The next morning, Ansel's father gave him a perfect gift: a simple box camera, the Kodak Brownie. Intrigued with his new toy, Ansel dashed off taking every picture in sight. Once, anxious to get a photo of the rock wall known as Half Dome, Ansel fell off a tree stump and took the picture upside down.

These first snapshots of Yosemite stirred Ansel's vision forever. He returned every summer of his life, at first working as a guide for the Sierra Club, a national nonprofit organization dedicated to protecting the environment. Soon, his pictures were in the Sierra Club newsletter. Then he spent four summers as a caretaker for a lodge owned by the Sierra Club. Gradually, Ansel learned the ways of hiking and mountain climbing. Hiking high in the Sierra Nevadas, he found splendid new views. He graduated from his Brownie to more demanding cameras and learned the special techniques needed to portray the magnificence of nature.

But picture-taking was merely a hobby, because officially, Adams was training to become a classical pianist. Yet, the young man found himself drawn more and more away from the keyboard and toward the camera. He assembled examples of his work in impressive photo portfolios. After a time, he reluctantly accepted the fact that his hands were too small for a professional piano player. Adams's mother was disappointed. She begged him to reconsider, remarking that the camera could never express the human soul. "Perhaps the camera cannot," he replied, "but the photographer can." So, in his late 20s, Ansel Adams abandoned his musical career and made up his mind to make photography his life's work.

CAREER HIGHLIGHTS

In a photography career spanning more than 50 years, Ansel Adams created breathtaking photographs of America's natural wonders — from sweeping vistas of glorious mountains to precise close-ups of a single flower. He also worked, at various times during his long career, as a commercial photographer, as a photography teacher, and as a writer. In addition, his love of nature led him to serve for 37 years, from 1936 to 1973, on the Board of Directors of the Sierra Club, helping in the fight to protect the environment.

EARLY CAREER

Adams's debut as a photographer came in 1927 with his first book of photographs, *Parmelian Prints of the High Sierras*. A year later, the Sierra Club exhibited his work. Adams had married by that point, and with a wife and two children to support, he often worked as a commercial photographer for businesses. Soon he began developing his own theories of photography, with special attention to the fundamentals of precision and sharpness. A natural teacher, he published a series of instructional books on the craft of photography. He also ran workshops and seminars in the Yosemite Valley and lectured at several California colleges and at New York's Museum of Modern Art. Adams traveled throughout the United States to lecture on his photographic philosophy of ultra clarity and classical grandeur, but it was his pictures of natural landscapes that made him famous.

TURNING POINT

The turning point in Adams's career was the founding in 1932 of a photographers' league called "Group f/64." Its motto was "make it sharp or don't make it at all." Determined to reverse the "soft focus" school of photography then popular, Adams and his colleagues chose sharp focus as their theme. They focused through f/64, the smallest opening in the camera's lens. This is the camera setting that yields the greatest depth of field and the ultimate in sharp clarity, from close-ups to longer views.

Yet, f/64 was more than a lens setting; it was a platform for high art. Adams used it to capture natural visual perfection: powerful surf rolling back to sea, twilight clouds moving across the sky, and the granite outcroppings of Mount McKinley, counterpointed by soft clouds. Adams was an expert climber who would hike high in the mountains for miles to find the best angle and best light for a photograph. "Sometimes I think I do get to places," he once said, "just when God is ready to have somebody click the shutter." Over the decades, Adams toured nearly every state to photograph its natural treasures. He carried a large view camera, a heavy wooden tripod, and a 40-pound backpack full of gear. Of course, Adams could not use the small roll-film camera that amateur snapshooters use. To get his precise scenic views, he used a large-view camera, which is about as big as a medium-sized television set (and almost as heavy). He put in one sheet of film at a time and focused by pulling back the rear of the camera with a bellows. He also used a very advanced lens to make the picture razor sharp.

FAMOUS PHOTOGRAPHS

Adams saw beauty everywhere in nature. He could photograph a single blade of grass wet with raindrops or a lonely desert cactus. But his most famous photographs are large black-and-white landscapes dramatizing the scenic grandeur of the American West. They are timeless. They could have been taken yesterday or 20,000 years ago.

Sometimes Adams hiked all day to get to the right spot at the right time to get his photographs. But his most famous picture was found just by chance. Driving on a back road near San Diego in 1941, exhausted after a day of uneventful shooting, Adams suddenly came upon a perfect picture. The moon was rising white in the east while a sinking sun in the west illuminated weather-worn white crosses in a church graveyard. Quickly, Adams set up his big camera on his tripod, guessed the correct exposure at one second, and pressed the shutter. By the time he got his second sheet of film loaded, it was too late—the sun had sunk into the hills. But he had gotten that first shot, and it was breathtaking. He called it *Moonrise*. When a large print of *Moonrise* sold for $71,500 at a Los Angeles gallery in 1981, it was the highest price ever paid for a work by a living photographer. At the time, Adams cracked, "Don't they know I'm not dead yet?"

ENVIRONMENTALIST AND HUMANITARIAN

Over the years, Adams used his fame and popularity to speak out about conservation and the environment. And he began this crusade decades before it was popular—long before most Americans understood the importance of preserving our environment. Time and again, he took his

Half Dome, Blowing Snow, Yosemite National Park, circa 1955

crusade to Washington, D.C. With his rough white beard and big Stetson hat, he was a showy figure on Capitol Hill, telling United States presidents and congressional leaders how important it was to protect the rugged Western landscapes. In 1940, when Congress was considering a national park in California's Kings Canyon, Adams's photos made the difference. When President Franklin Roosevelt saw the pictures, he convinced Congress to preserve Kings Canyon. In 1980, President Jimmy Carter awarded Adams the Presidential Medal of Freedom, the nation's highest civilian award. President Carter said: "It is through his foresight and fortitude that so much of America has been saved for future Americans."

With his camera, Adams showed why nature is worth saving. But while he had deep respect for the earth, he also had compassion for the people who walk on it. For example, during World War II, 100,000 Japanese-Americans were ordered by the United States government to be placed in detention camps. The war with Japan had stirred strong fears regarding national security, and some people believed that Japanese-Americans would betray their country. Adams, mindful of the plight of such minority groups, published *Born Free and Equal* in 1944, an eloquent photographic portfolio of a stark California camp used to intern Japanese-Americans.

LEGACY

"In a career that spanned more than 50 years," John Russell wrote in the *New York Times*, "Mr. Adams combined a passion for landscape, meticulous craftsmanship as a printmaker, and a missionary's zeal for his medium to become the most widely exhibited and recognized photographer of his generation. . . . In addition to being acclaimed for his dramatic landscapes of the American West, he was held in high esteem for his contributions to photographic technology and to the recognition of photography as an art form."

In one magnificent photograph after another, Ansel Adams captured the natural glories of the United States. He did it through the brilliance of his photographic technique. In many writings, he noted the importance of photographic vision, as opposed to gadgetry. "A picture is only a collection of brightnesses," he once wrote. Yet "there is nothing worse than a brilliant image of a fuzzy concept."

While other photographers of his time chased after shocking and sensational pictures, Adams mastered the everyday skills of photographic realism, faithfully documenting the real world. A master of his craft, he often worked for days to develop a perfect print. Remembering his training in classical music, Adams once said, "The negative is like a score in music. The print is the performance." Adams found creative excitement in the darkroom. With an enlarger, he would lighten or darken different areas of the picture or select the best section of it. Photographers call this process "dodging," "burning in," and "cropping." Adams also developed what he called the "zone system" of calculating exposure. This system is used to control contrast in the negative by dividing light and dark areas into ten shades, or "zones," of gray.

Adams the artist marched hand in hand with Adams the environmentalist. He saw his mission as capturing the scenic wonders of America before commercial development overtook the land. "It was his good fortune to survey God's country before God stood aside and the developers came pouring in," wrote Richard Lacayo in *Time* magazine. "He worked with the deepening sense that time was running out for the landscape he loved."

"As a photographer Adams was an undisputed master of the natural landscape," Judy Dater wrote in *Contemporary Photographers*. "With clarity and precision he portrayed and heightened the spectacular vistas and rich native details of the western United States. Rivers, mountains, valleys, orchards, deserts and sea — all are chronicled, and fused with his poetic vision and his conservation instincts. 'My approach to photography [Adams wrote] is based on my belief in the vigor and values of the world of nature — in the aspects of grandeur and of the minutiae all about us.'"

Adams believed that the future of the American landscape was linked to the future of the nation. His photographs became the symbols for Americans determined to retain the natural wilderness that is America's treasure. For him, the conservation of nature was almost a religion. Adams believed in the power of nature to replenish the human spirit. "Some people belong to a church," he once said. "Conservation is my point of focus."

Adams's photographic legacy in a way also created problems, however. By presenting natural wonders in their most idealized state, Adams lured countless Americans to the area to share in the treasures he had documented. Millions of tourists came to see these natural wonders for themselves, turning the national parks into traffic jams of cars and people. "His delectable pictures brought mobs of tourists to his beloved Yosemite," wrote art critic Douglas Davis in *Newsweek* magazine, "filling the valleys and streams with Coca-Cola bottles and ice-cream cups." Nonetheless, Davis concluded, if Adams failed to make the world see and act as he wished, "he left an immutable record of it behind. His pictures preserve moments from a time that would otherwise be lost."

Adams died of heart disease on April 22, 1984, near his home in Carmel, California, where he moved after leaving Yosemite Valley in 1962. Quite fittingly, his ashes were scattered over Yosemite, from a peak christened Mount Ansel Adams.

MARRIAGE AND FAMILY

Adams met his future wife, Virginia Best, in 1921. Virginia was the daughter of Harry Cassie Best, an artist with a studio in Yosemite. Adams and Virginia soon fell in love, but they were too young to marry. Eventually, after a dramatic Christmastime proposal by Adams, they decided to marry. A few days later, on January 2, 1928, they were wed in her father's studio by a local minister. They had two children, Michael and Anne, and five grandchildren.

SELECTED WORKS

Parmelian Prints of the High Sierras, 1927
Making a Photograph, 1935
Born Free and Equal: The Story of Loyal Japanese-Americans at Manzanar Relocation Center, 1944
Ansel Adams Basic Photo Series:
  Camera and Lens, 1948
  The Negative, 1948
  The Print, 1950
  Natural Light Photography, 1952
  Artificial Light Photography, 1956

Images 1923-1974, 1975
Yosemite and the Range of Light, 1979
Examples: The Making of 40 Photographs, 1983
Ansel Adams: An Autobiography, 1985 (with Mary Street Alinder)
Letters and Images 1916-1984, 1988

HONORS AND AWARDS

Guggenheim Fellowship: 1946, 1948
Brehm Memorial Award (Rochester Institute of Technology): 1958
John Muir Award (Sierra Club): 1962
Fellow of the American Academy of Arts and Sciences: 1966
Conservation Service award (United States Department of the Interior):
   1968
Progress Medal (Photographic Society of America): 1969
Chubb Fellow (Yale University): 1970
Special Citation (American Institute of Architects): 1971
Ansel Adams Conservation Award (The Wilderness Society): 1980
Presidential Medal of Freedom: 1980

FURTHER READING

BOOKS

Adams, Ansel, with Mary Street Alinder. *Ansel Adams: An Autobiography,*
   1985
Contemporary Photographers, 1995
Encyclopedia Americana, 1992
Encyclopedia Britannica, 1991
Newhall, Nancy Wynne. *Ansel Adams: The Eloquent Light,* 1963
Who Was Who, Vol. VII
World Book Encyclopedia, 1994
Wrigley, Richard. *Ansel Adams: Images of the American West,* 1992

PERIODICALS

ARTNews, Summer 1984, p.76
Atlantic, Oct. 1985, p.99
Boys' Life, July 1994, p.28
MacLean's, May 7, 1984, p.7
Newsweek, Sep. 24, 1979, p.90; May 7, 1984, p.106
New York Times, Apr. 24, 1984, p.B6; Apr. 25, 1984, p.C15
Reader's Digest, Mar. 1980, p.139
Time, Sep. 3, 1979, p.36; May 7, 1984, p.124; Sep. 3, 1990, p.62

OBITUARY

Romare Bearden   1912?-1988
American Artist
Pioneering Creator of Collage Art Depicting
the African-American Experience

BIRTH

Romare Howard Bearden was born in Charlotte, North
Carolina, on September 2. His year of birth was probably
1912, although some sources give 1911 or 1914 as the year.
His father, Richard Bearden, was an accomplished pianist,
who later worked as a sanitation inspector for the Department of Health in New York City. Romare's grandfather and

great-grandfather on his father's side were both artists. His mother, Bessye (Johnson) Bearden, was the founder and first president of the Negro Women's Democratic Association and worked as the New York correspondent for a regional African-American newspaper, the *Chicago Defender*. An only child, Romare was nicknamed "Romie" by family and close friends.

YOUTH

Romare Bearden's earliest experiences were of the sights and sounds of the rural South: railroad trains coming and going, farmhands working in the fields, women sewing patchwork quilts. His parents moved to the Harlem section of New York City when Bearden was about 5 years old, but all through his childhood years he continued to spend summers with his paternal grandparents and great-grandparents in rural Mecklenburg County, North Carolina, and later on with a grandmother in Baltimore, Maryland. Music, especially blues and jazz, was a part of Bearden's everyday life as far back as he could remember. He vividly recalled his father's playing piano duets with such great musicians as Fats Waller and Duke Ellington in his parents' apartment in Harlem.

When he was about 13, Bearden went to live in Pittsburgh, Pennsylvania, for a while with his maternal grandmother, who ran a boardinghouse there. Many of the boarders were recent migrants from the South, and Bearden liked to listen to them playing guitar and singing "down home" blues. There he became friends with Eugene Bailey, a boy his own age who loved to draw pictures, and Romare began to do some pencil sketches of his own. Interested in everything around him, he also enjoyed reading books and writing letters, and he took an active interest in sports. When his friend Eugene suddenly died of illness, Romare attended the funeral. The old-fashioned gospel church service and burial ceremony was one of the saddest and most moving moments of his youth.

EDUCATION

Bearden completed his elementary school education at New York's Public School 139 in Harlem in 1925 and graduated from Peabody High School in Pittsburgh in 1929. He played sports throughout these years, becoming particularly good at baseball while in high school. He took a break from school for two years, and then attended New York University from 1931 to 1935. He entered college as a pre-medical student in mathematics, since his mother hoped he would become a doctor. He earned a bachelor's degree in mathematics in 1935. During 1936-37, Bearden attended classes at the Art Students League in Manhattan. Years later, from 1950 to 1951, he went to France and studied philosophy at the Sorbonne in Paris.

CHOOSING A CAREER

Bearden tried several different careers on his way to becoming an artist. After finishing high school in Pittsburgh, Bearden played professional baseball in the Negro Leagues as a pitcher with the Boston Tigers (1930-31). At this time, baseball, like many activities in American life, was segregated by race. African-Americans were not allowed to play in the whites-only major leagues, so talented African-Americans played in the lower-paying Negro leagues. Since he had a light complexion, Bearden was told he could probably pass for white and make it as a player in the major leagues, but he was extremely uncomfortable with and resentful of such an idea. He left baseball after two seasons.

Uncertain about his plans, it was then that Bearden entered New York University as a math major. While in college, he drew cartoons and editorial sketches for the *NYU Medley*, the students' humor magazine. He also earned a little money selling drawings to the *Baltimore Afro-American* newspaper and the well-known magazines *Collier's* and the *Saturday Evening Post*.

After his college graduation in 1935, Bearden began attending meetings of African-American artists and writers at the Harlem YMCA and joined an informal group of artists who met at the studio of his cousin, painter Charles Alston. Coming into contact with so many creative people in the Harlem community, including such young hopefuls as painter Jacob Lawrence and novelist Ralph Ellison, encouraged Bearden to think seriously about making art his career. In 1935 he began taking classes at the Art Students League taught by George Grosz, a German social protest painter who had recently fled the Nazi government that had taken over his native country. During this time, Bearden experimented with various painting styles. In 1937, he exhibited a few paintings in a group show at the Harlem YMCA. But he was unable at the time to support himself by his art, so he took a job as a social worker with the New York City Department of Social Services and did painting during his hours after work. Some of his early works were exhibited in a small one-man show in Harlem in 1940 and in group shows of African-American artists elsewhere in the city the following year. His scenes depicting life in the South, such as *Two Women in a Landscape* (1941), have the flavor of African sculpture with their plain, strong forms and earthy colors.

Then in April 1942, a few months after the United States entered World War II, Bearden was drafted into the United States Army. He served with the all-black 372nd Infantry Regiment in Europe, earned the rank of sergeant, and was discharged in May 1945. Bearden went back to his job in New York as a social worker and started painting again.

CAREER HIGHLIGHTS

Highly gifted, with a brilliant, inquiring mind and the ability to paint or draw in a great many different ways, Bearden kept searching throughout his career for styles in which he could fully express himself. He incorporated many different influences and experimented with a variety of approaches during his long career.

Bearden started out with his first major one-man show at the Kootz Gallery in New York in October 1945, shortly after his return from the war. This show featured a series of paintings based on the New Testament called The Passion of Christ. These paintings were done in a modern "cubist" style, in which the objects shown were transformed into such geometric shapes as cubes, squares, and triangles. Such paintings as his *Madonna and Child* (1945) contained figures made up of geometric forms in bold combinations that viewers found powerful, direct, and very moving. Almost all of these paintings were sold. In other shows over the next few years, Bearden used the same techniques to create mournful, tragic scenes based on poems by modern Spanish poet Federico Garcia Lorca; lively pictures making fun of everyday life suggested by the writings of 16th-century French author Francois Rabelais; and scenes of the Trojan War from the ancient Greek poem *The Iliad*. By 1949, Bearden was recognized as an important American modern artist and his paintings were being included in exhibitions all across the country.

Still restless and searching, however, and unwilling to rest on his reputation, Bearden decided to use his veterans' education benefits in 1950 to go and study philosophy at the University of Paris (the Sorbonne). While in Paris, Bearden met such famous modern European artists and sculptors as Pablo Picasso, Georges Braque, and Constantin Brancusi. He also became acquainted with a number of African writers there, among them the Senegalese poet Leopold Sedar Senghor, who 20 years later became the president of Senegal. These overseas encounters broadened Bearden's thinking about art and life and deepened his sense of identity as an African-American as well.

EXPERIMENTING WITH MUSIC AND ART

Upon his return from France in 1951, Bearden rented a studio in Harlem over the Apollo Theater on West 125th Street. But for the next several years, he stopped painting altogether. In the meantime, Bearden got his old job back as a social worker. He also returned to his love of music and began to write jazz tunes and lyrics, and he succeeded in publishing quite a few. One of them, "Sea Breeze," was recorded by jazz artists Billy Eckstein, Oscar Pettiford, and Dizzy Gillespie, and became a hit. In 1954, to find his way back to his art again, Bearden began by painting practice copies of works by such old masters as Rembrandt and Eugene Delacroix, among others, and such great modern artists as Henri Matisse and Picasso. These exercises led him to experiment with an approach to art then in fashion known as "abstract expressionism," which originated in New York City in the 1940s. Artists who worked in this style were rebelling against old forms of "literal" or landscape art and used blobs of paint or bold strokes of color to create abstract designs on canvas.

For Bearden, this was a fascinating way to go even further in searching out his feelings about art, to make new discoveries about color and space, and to create a wider range of emotional moods and effects. Just as in his first, early works and then his series of modern cubist paintings, Bearden's originality came through in this newer abstract expressionist style as well. For the next five or six years, painting by instinct and intuition, he produced serene, dreamlike compositions with shifting colors and forms. Bearden had several one-man shows of his abstract art during these years at the Barone Gallery, the Michael Warren Gallery, and Cordier & Warren in New York City. Critics admired Bearden's new freedom in such works as *Mountains of the Moon* (1956), *The Mirror* (1959), and *Blue Is the Smoke of War, White the Bones of Men* (1960), among many others.

By the early 1960s, Bearden had worked and struggled through a great many different approaches in his art and had won a good deal of recognition. Now, at the age of 50, he began turning out works that are today regarded by many as his most important and original accomplishments. By 1963, the civil-rights movement had started to gain momentum. Members of the movement sought to increase the rights of African-Americans and to end discrimination based on race. Bearden organized a meeting with a number of African-American artists and writers at his new studio in lower Manhattan to talk about what they could do. After their discussion, Bearden decided that now was the time for him to try and capture his personal and cultural identity as an African-American in his art. When he was a young man just starting out as an artist back in the 1930s, Bearden had attempted to deal with this theme in the "social realist" style common to that time. Social realism incorporated political and social issues into art that was rendered in a highly realistic manner. Now, however, Bearden turned to quite a different artistic style, the "collage," in which an artist pastes pieces of paper or cloth, cutouts of photographs, clippings from magazines or newspapers, and all sorts of other materials on a board or other flat surface to create a work of art. As it turned out, in Bearden's hands the medium of collage was raised to a new, higher level of expression, as he portrayed African-American life in a striking visual language rarely before seen in American art.

Evening: 9:10, 461 Lenox Avenue, 1964

SUCCESS WITH COLLAGES

Bearden's first collages, mostly done in black-and-white and various shades of gray, were also called "photo montages" because he used cutouts from photographs of water, cloth, wood, leaves, grass, and sheet metal to put together his shapes. When he was finished, he had the completed works photographically enlarged to many times their original size. About 30 photo montages were exhibited, with their smaller originals alongside, at the Cordier & Ekstrom Gallery in New York City in 1964, and a second group a year later at the Corcoran Gallery in Washington, D.C. Based upon all his memories and experiences from early childhood onward, they dealt with African-American life in Charlotte, Pittsburgh, and Harlem. Some, like *Baptism* (1964), dealt with communal churchgoing. Others depicted city street scenes or people in their apartments, as in *Evening: 9:10, 461 Lenox Avenue* (1964), and still others, such as *Cotton* (1964), showed sharecroppers picking cotton in the fields in the South. These works received wide attention and praise from scholars, critics, and the general public. Finally, Bearden was able to make a living as a professional artist. In 1966, he left his job as a social worker to devote himself to his art full-time.

For the next 20 years, Bearden created works based almost entirely on African-American themes. He turned out pieces much larger than his first collages and added colored materials to go along with the black-and-white cutouts. Bearden also began to use a lot of paint, making his works just as much paintings as they were collages. A number of common images kept showing up in Bearden's art. Railroad trains, a symbol of migration and the wider world outside recalled from his childhood, appear in *Watching the Good Trains Go By* (1964), *The Visitor* (1976), and *Southern Limited* (1976), among others. The image of the "conjure woman," an old, wise woman traditionally held in esteem and awe in African-American communities for her power to heal, tell fortunes, and cast spells, is seen in several works. Jazz scenes and images of black people and blues guitar players depict the important place of music in the everyday life and tradition. "Of the Blues," an exhibition of 20 Bearden works in this theme, was held in New York City in 1975. Bearden also did a number of images of women in private scenes of nude or partly nude figures that have a quiet, magical feeling. Among these are *Madam's White Bird* (1975), *The Living Room* (1978), and *Storyville* (1979). One of Bearden's largest painted collages, *The Block* (1971), is like a movie set. Measuring 4 by 18 feet, accompanied by a sound track of gospel and blues, children's voices, and street sounds, it reproduces life on a city block in Harlem just as if viewers were right there themselves. "What I've attempted to do," Bearden once said of his painted collages, "is establish a world through art in which the validity of my Negro experience could live." Those who view Bearden's collages conclude that he succeeded.

Farewell Eugene (1978), a particularly sad and moving funeral scene remembering the childhood friend who inspired him to draw, is representative of many of Bearden's collages. The eyes, faces, hands, arms, and legs of the mourners, pieced together out of photographic cutouts of people of all kinds, from different times and places, seem to give the figures at the crowded ceremony a sense of history and cultural continuity from generation to generation in the African-American heritage. One of Bearden's last works, done in 1986, was a large mosaic mural, measuring 10 by 13 feet, made up of brightly colored pieces of glass instead of paper cutouts. Titled *Quilting Time*, it shows a group of African-American women making a patchwork quilt together. The subject was a direct reference to his own style of work. "After all," Bearden said, "working in collage was precisely what the ladies were doing." A year later, he was awarded the National Medal of the Arts. Bearden died in New York City on March 12, 1988.

MAJOR INFLUENCES

Bearden's work demonstrates a broad range of influences from the entire world history of art, from ancient times to the present. His works contain structure, visual elements, and techniques that he gained over a lifetime of experience and study. African sculpture can be seen in many of Bearden's faces and figures. Ways to combine grays with bright colors he learned from the ancient Roman wall paintings of the destroyed city of Pompeii. Some of his people, as in *Family* (1967) and *She-ba* (1970), look like ancient Egyptian or Greek figures. Other works, such as *Patchwork Quilt* (1969), combine rectangles from the style of the modern abstract painter Piet Mondrian with layouts similar to the 17th-century Dutch painter Jan Vermeer. A simple work like *Black Mother and Child* (1970) has the flavor of an ancient Byzantine painting or an altarpiece from the Middle Ages. The Chinese and Japanese use of flat planes and empty space in their paintings are also present in some of Bearden's work. At the same time, Bearden found that listening to jazz while he worked, especially the recordings of pianist Earl Hines, helped give a musical feeling to his paintings.

Bearden's openness to different cultures and traditions of art, literature, and civilization helped him to appreciate the richness of his own heritage. In order to find things in the African-American experience to make into art, Bearden once remarked about himself, "I did not need to do more than look out of my studio window above the Apollo Theater on 125th Street."

MARRIAGE AND FAMILY

In 1954, Bearden married Nanette Rohan, who was born on the Caribbean island of St. Martin in the French West Indies. They had no children. A dancer and an artist, Rohan was the organizer of the New York City Chamber Dance Company. Her encouragement helped Bearden get back into his art during the time in the early 1950s when he had nearly stopped painting altogether. During most of their marriage, the couple divided their time each year between New York City and their home out on St. Martin. As a result, Bearden produced many colorful scenes of Caribbean life in addition to his other works.

HOBBIES AND OTHER INTERESTS

Bearden was a visual artist, a baseball player, a composer of songs, and an author as well. He wrote several books about his own approach to art and also about the works and careers of many other African-American artists. In addition, he also helped African-American art to become better known by organizing major exhibits in Harlem and elsewhere and by setting up gallery spaces for younger artists to display their works. After his death, Nanette Bearden helped to administer a trust fund he had set up, the Romare Bearden Foundation, to assist talented young art students.

WRITINGS

The Painter's Mind, 1969 (with Carl Holty)
Six Black Masters in American Art, 1972 (with Harry Henderson)
The Caribbean Poetry of Derek Walcott and the Art of Romare Bearden, 1983
   (with Derek Walcott)
A History of African-American Artists, 1993 (with Harry Henderson)

HONORS AND AWARDS

American Academy and Institute of Arts and Letters: 1966
John Simon Guggenheim Memorial Fellowship: 1970
Ford Foundation Fellowship: 1973
Frederick Douglass Medal (New York Urban League): 1978
James Weldon Johnson Award (National Association for the
   Advancement of Colored People): 1978
National Medal of Arts (National Endowment for he Arts): 1987

FURTHER READING

BOOKS

Brown, Kevin. *Romare Bearden*, 1995 (juvenile)
Contemporary Artists, 1996
Encyclopedia Americana, 1995
Encyclopedia Britannica, 1995
Fax, Elton C. *Seventeen Black Artists*, 1971
Schwartzman, Myron. *Romare Bearden: His Life and Art*, 1990
Washington, Bunch M. *The Art of Romare Bearden: The Prevalence
   of Ritual*, 1973
Who Was Who, Vol. IX
World Book Encyclopedia, 1996

PERIODICALS

Art in America, Dec. 1981, p.134
ARTNews, Oct. 1964, p.24; Dec. 1980, p.60; Summer 1988, p.40;
   Feb. 1992, p.21
Current Biography Yearbook 1972; 1988 (obituary)
New York, May 13, 1991, p.99
New York Times, Jan. 3, 1987, Section 1, p.15; Jan. 2, 1987, Section 2, p.33;
   Mar. 13, 1988, Section 1, p.36; Mar. 27, 1988, Section 2, p.41; Apr. 19,
   1991, p.C26
Newsweek, Apr. 29, 1991, p.58
Smithsonian, Mar. 1981, p.70
Time, Mar. 28, 1988, p.69; June 10, 1991, p.134

OBITUARY

Margaret Bourke-White   1904-1971
American Photographer
Photojournalist of American Industry and
World War II

BIRTH

Margaret White, later known as Margaret Bourke-White,
was born in New York City on June 14, 1904. Her parents,
Joseph White and Minnie Elizabeth (Bourke) White, raised
their children as Christians, even though Joseph, an engineer
and inventor, came from an Orthodox Jewish family. Their
child-rearing approach also derived from the weekly meet-

ings they attended of the Ethical Culture movement, which promoted strict moral values and hard work. Margaret was the second of their three children, with an older sister, Ruth, and a younger brother, Roger.

YOUTH

Bourke-White grew up in a suburb of New York City called Bound Brook, New Jersey, near the factory where her father worked developing new types of printing presses. Her home life was filled with intellectual stimulation — books were everywhere — and her mother read to the children every day when they were young. Both Joseph and Minnie fostered a love of nature in their children. Joseph took his children for long walks in the neighboring Watchung Mountains, where he identified the birds, insects, plants, and, at night, the constellations. At home, her father was a silent presence, always thinking, totally absorbed in his work. Margaret was his favorite because she was so inquisitive and because she adored him.

EARLY MEMORIES

Bourke-White was fearful as a child, and her parents were determined to help her develop a sense of courage. To temper her fear of being in the house alone, her mother would create a game out of leaving the house for awhile, gradually lengthening the time in which Bourke-White was alone until finally the little girl was no longer afraid. Meanwhile, her father helped calm her fears of certain animals, especially snakes, by identifying all the snakes they encountered on their walks in the woods and picking up the nonpoisonous ones until Bourke-White could hold these snakes by herself. Her father built cages for the snakes and all the other wildlife she brought home. She learned to like snakes so much that she planned on becoming a herpetologist, a person who studies reptiles and amphibians. In her autobiography, *Portrait of Myself* (1963), she recalled how, as a little girl, she would dream of becoming a scientist, traveling all over the world studying reptiles and bringing back specimens to the natural history museums — in other words, "doing all the things that women never do."

Trying to get more attention, she would bring her snakes to school, wrapped around her shoulders, a behavior that often landed her in the principal's office. Although she certainly was noticed for her unique talents, she was not particularly popular, and all during high school she never once went out on a date. She later attributed her difficult adolescence to her parents' strict, Victorian code of behavior and dress for their children. Bourke-White was not allowed to chew gum, play cards, read newspaper comics, eat white bread or fried foods, or go to the movies with other children. In hindsight, Bourke-White recognized that what her parents gave her — a love of truth and honesty and a striving for perfection — was "perhaps the most valuable inheritance a child could receive."

MAJOR INFLUENCES

As much as Bourke-White loved her mother, she rejected the choices she had made in her life. Bourke-White was determined to be more active in the world and not resign herself to the domestic chores of a traditional wife and mother. Her role model was her father. An amateur photographer, Joseph White was fascinated by the science of optics, the study of the transmission and control of light, and he was always experimenting with new lenses or prisms. Bourke-White would follow him around, observing everything he did and asking endless questions, which he always answered. She considered herself his chief assistant, often staging photo opportunities for him and helping him in the darkroom. However, it was not until years later, after he died when she was 18 years old, that Bourke-White first picked up a camera.

Sometimes, she accompanied him on his business trips where he would oversee the installation of his printing presses. When she was eight years old, she went with her father to a foundry that was manufacturing the printing press that he had recently invented. This experience made a lasting impression on her. She recalled in her autobiography how she watched in awe as the dark foundry became alive with the heat and glow of the flowing metal — the sparks flew everywhere. "I can hardly describe my joy. To me, at that age, a foundry represented the beginning and end of all beauty. Later when I became a photographer . . . this memory was so vivid and so alive that it shaped the whole course of my career."

EDUCATION

Bourke-White's early schooling was in New Jersey. She did well in high school, where her favorite subjects were English and biology. She edited the yearbook, acted in school plays, presided over the drama club, and participated in the debating society. Bourke-White started college in 1922 at Columbia University in New York City. What happened during her first Christmas vacation changed her life forever. Her beloved father, at the age of 51, suffered a massive stroke and died within 24 hours. Because she was so grief-stricken over his death, Bourke-White started playing with the cameras that she had watched him work with during her entire childhood. She returned to Columbia and took photography courses from a master photographer, Clarence White, who taught her to think of photographs as works of art and to compose them as an artist would compose a painting. Yet herpetology had been her chosen career, and she transferred in 1923 to the University of Michigan in Ann Arbor to study with a famous zoologist, Alexander Ruthven.

In 1925, Bourke-White married Everett Chapman, whom she had met at the University of Michigan. She moved around with her engineer husband and took courses in paleontology, the study of plant and animal fossils, at Rutgers University in New Jersey, at Purdue University in Indiana, and at Case Western Reserve University in Ohio. Bourke-White's marriage proved to be short lived, though. Having separated from her husband in 1926, she applied to Cornell University in Ithaca, New York, to complete her senior year studying zoology. She graduated with a bachelor's degree from Cornell in 1927.

CHOOSING A CAREER

It was during her college years that Bourke-White decided to become a photographer. Her father's death left the family with little money. They had lived rather comfortably off of his salary, but he had left no savings or insurance. So Bourke-White was forced to work during college, a circumstance that actually set the stage for her decision to become a professional photographer. As she was unable to get any traditional work, primarily because all the part-time jobs on campus were taken by the time she applied, she was forced to rely on her wits to earn money.

When she was at the University of Michigan, she took photographs of the college campus and found that other students liked them and wanted to buy them. Seeing a good opportunity, she set up a card table outside of the cafeteria and sold her pictures. Bourke-White soon became skilled at getting people to help market her photographs. When it came to photography, she was outgoing and passionate, qualities that endeared her to her peers and that would later help her in the business world. She continued to sell her photographs when she attended Cornell, which led to her pictures being printed in the school newspaper and magazine.

Bourke-White was encouraged to become an architectural photographer by many of the Cornell alumni, who saw her photographs in their magazine. As she was uncertain whether her photographs were that valuable outside of the college campus, she brought a portfolio of her work to one of New York's finest architects, Benjamin Moscowitz. He confirmed what the Cornell alumni had told her — she could work for any architectural firm in the country because her pictures were that good. This was the magic moment for her. Now she knew she would be a professional photographer.

CAREER HIGHLIGHTS

Bourke-White's entry into professional photography was as an independent, or freelance, photographer. She took pictures of what she liked and tried to sell them. After graduating from Cornell in 1927, she returned to Cleveland, a city she loved for its sprawling and photogenic industrial sections. Over the next few years, she established herself in the field of photography.

Bourke-White began using the hyphenated form of her name when she established a photography business, the Bourke-White Studio, in 1927. She took her mother's maiden name and hyphenated it with her father's name, which was extremely unusual for that time. In those first years, she operated on a tight budget — the classic struggling artist. She used her two-room apartment where she lived and slept as the base for her business and also as her darkroom, developing prints in the kitchen sink and rinsing them in the bathtub. Her first big break came in the form of an assignment from her Cornell connections to photograph a new school built by several Cornell alumni. This photograph was printed in a national architectural magazine and led to a steady stream of work.

One day in 1928, as she walked through a park in downtown Cleveland, Bourke-White saw a preacher on a pedestal whose only audience was a flock of pigeons. She was dying to take a picture, but she did not have her camera with her. She ran into a nearby camera store and begged the owner to let her borrow a camera for this perfect picture. She bought a bag of peanuts for passersby to throw to keep the pigeons on the ground in front of the preacher. This picture was featured on the cover of a local magazine. Even more fortunate for her was the fact that the camera shop owner, Alfred Hall Bemis, became a close friend and adviser. He helped her solve many of her technical problems, and he let her use his equipment and darkroom. He guided her to follow her own heart and photograph what she wanted, not what anyone else wanted.

Her next big break came during the late 1920s with a monthly assignment from the Union Trust Bank. The bank used one of her industrial photos every month for the cover of its monthly magazine. She was paid $50 a month, a large amount of money for that time, and a particularly large sum for a photograph. Encouraged by her success with the bank, she drove to Otis Steel to meet with its president. Her goal was to photograph the interior of Otis's massive factory in a way that would show its grandeur and beauty. At first, the president of the company questioned her perception of the steel mill as something artistic and failed to see the value of such photographs. Bourke-White explained that the steel mill represented the new industrial age of the United States and, as a symbol of hope for the future, was an object of beauty. The company president was impressed with her logic and agreed to allow her free access to the interior of the steel mill.

Bourke-White spent every night for months taking pictures at the steel mill with her good friend Alfred Bemis. It was a great challenge to be able to photograph the bright molten steel against the great blackness of the mill's interior. There were countless technical problems that she and Bemis had to overcome. Ultimately, though, she succeeded. Her photographs were widely published and met with great acclaim. Bourke-White had established her trademark in the field of photography and had become famous.

PHOTOGRAPHER FOR *FORTUNE* MAGAZINE

Henry Luce, publisher of *Time* magazine, was fascinated with Bourke-White's pictures of the Otis Steel mill and hired her, in 1929, to help illustrate his new magazine, *Fortune*. He wanted *Fortune* to capture the spirit of the modern industrial world. However, it was not her pictures of steel that covered the pages of the first *Fortune* magazine, but her pictures of Chicago slaughterhouses and of hogs being butchered. This issue caught the eye of wealthy American business leaders as well as patrons of the arts. Bourke-White became more than famous — she became a star.

Her personal style drew as much attention as did her dramatic photographs. She was often the object of another photographer's camera lens, being photographed perched at the top of the Chrysler Building in New York City trying to take a picture, dangling from a plane, or dancing in nightclubs. Bourke-White, who had been born slightly afraid of the world, was no longer fearful. She would go anywhere and do anything.

Bourke-White's work was featured in *Fortune* magazine for the next seven years. She traveled to Germany and to the Soviet Union (now Russia) to photograph their factories and big industries. Meanwhile, she also had advertising clients such as Buick and Goodyear. Because she never turned down work, she was incredibly busy, and she earned a lot of money. But the "Dust Bowl" drought of 1934 changed the direction of her photography. The term "Dust Bowl" describes parts of the Great Plains in the United States and Canada. The area earned that name when enormous windstorms swept across dry grasslands and carried away the fertile topsoil, leaving the land too barren to be farmed. Photographing the desperate plight of the farmers who were forced to abandon their land affected Bourke-White so deeply that she could no longer photograph objects for advertising purposes. She became a full-time photojournalist. For the next few years, she toured the country with her camera, capturing the faces of the downtrodden and poor in America with her future husband, author Erskine Caldwell. Her photographs in their collaborative effort, *You Have Seen Their Faces*, showed the desolation of rural poverty during the Depression.

LIFE MAGAZINE PHOTOGRAPHER

In 1936, Henry Luce started another magazine, called *Life*, with a format that primarily featured pictures instead of words. Bourke-White went to work for *Life* and provided the cover photograph for the first issue. It was a study in geometric shapes of the construction in Montana of Fort

Peck Dam, which was, at the time, the largest earth-filled dam in the world. She was soon sent all over the world to take photographs for *Life*, in the Arctic, Central Europe, and all over the United States.

When World War II began, Bourke-White became the first female war photojournalist. She captured many shocking images of World War II in North Africa and Europe in the 1940s. Accredited by the U.S. Army Air Force, she was the first woman ever officially assigned to accompany the troops on raids. During the war, she was torpedoed off North Africa, flew on American bombing raids in Tunis, and rode with an artillery spotter in Italy. She was fearless. She covered the fighting in the Soviet Union and the Nazi attack on Moscow. She considered her photographs of the German nighttime bombing raids during the 1942 siege of Moscow to be some of her best work. Others, though, give that credit to her work of 1945. Assigned to cover the Third Army headed up by Lieut. Gen. George C. Patton, she took pictures at the liberation of Buchenwald, a Nazi concentration camp. Her stark photographs of the Nazi victims at Buchenwald stirred horror, outrage, and revulsion in the United States and around the world.

Buchenwald prisoners, 1945

After the war ended, Bourke-White continued to work for *Life*, traveling to India to cover that country's struggle for independence. She stayed there for almost two years and gained enormous respect for Mohandas Gandhi, the leader of the movement that used nonviolent civil disobedience in the struggle for India's independence from Great Britain. She then went to South Africa to produce some spectacular photographs of the effects of apartheid. This was a policy of racial segregation and discrimination against non-whites that was, at the time, enforced by the white minority government of South Africa. Bourke-White also captured the terrible working and living conditions of the black miners.

DIAGNOSED WITH PARKINSON'S DISEASE

While she was on assignment for *Life* to cover the Korean War (1950-53), Bourke-White noticed an ache in her left leg. She soon had trouble walking. She returned to the United States, and in 1953 she was diagnosed with Parkinson's disease, a neurological disorder that causes the body to shake uncontrollably. By the time she was 53 years old, in 1957, Bourke-White was forced to leave *Life* magazine because of the disabling effects of the disease. She retired to her home in Darien, Connecticut, where she worked on her autobiography until 1963. With another famous photographer and close friend, Alfred Eisenstadt, Bourke-White compiled a story for *Life* magazine about Parkinson's disease. She died on August 27, 1971, after a fall.

LEGACY

Creative, relentless, and fearless, Bourke-White was one of the first photojournalists and one of the world's pre-eminent photographers. Her legacy to the field was summed up by Eisenstadt, who paid her this tribute after her death: "[Bourke-White] was great because there was no assignment, no picture, that was unimportant to her. She immersed herself in the smallest detail, and everything she did was a challenge to her." Bourke-White would have agreed. She once revealed the secret of her work, saying "the camera is a remarkable instrument. Saturate yourself with your subject and the camera will all but take you by the hand."

MARRIAGE AND FAMILY

Bourke-White was married twice. In 1925, she married Everett Chapman, an engineer she had met at the University of Michigan. Chapman in many ways reminded her of her father. What had begun as a passionate love affair soon turned into an unhappy marriage, especially for Margaret. Besides having to deal with a hostile mother-in-law, she found herself smothered by a demanding husband who was jealous of her separate interests. When the marriage ended after less than two years, Margaret Bourke-White was determined to make it on her own.

In 1935, she was looking for a writer to help her with a book on Americans who had faced enormous difficulties during the economic decline of the Great Depression. At the same time, Erskine Caldwell, an established writer, was looking for a photographer to illustrate his book on the poor in America. They met and were a perfect match. They married in 1939 after living together for several years. During their time together, they collaborated on many books and shared the excitement of their respective professions. But as Bourke-White gained confidence in her own writing style, she pursued the book *Shooting the Russian War* as a solitary venture, which upset her husband. They divorced in 1942. She wrote of their marriage, "We had five good productive years with occasional tempests, it's true, but with some real happiness. I was relieved it was all over, and glad we parted with mutual affection and respect that still endures." Although Bourke-White desperately wanted a daughter, she never had any children.

SELECTED WRITINGS AND PUBLISHED COLLECTIONS

Eyes on Russia, 1931
You Have Seen Their Faces, 1937 (with Erskine Caldwell)
North of the Danube, 1939 (with Erskine Caldwell)
Say, Is This the U.S.A.?, 1941 (with Erskine Caldwell)
Shooting the Russian War, 1943
They Called It "Purple Heart Valley," 1944
"Dear Fatherland, Rest Quietly," 1946
Halfway to Freedom: A Study of the New India, 1949
A Report on the American Jesuits, 1956 (with John LaFarge)
Portrait of Myself, 1963

HONORS AND AWARDS

Carl Van Anda Award (Scripps School of Journalism, Ohio University): 1969
National Women's Hall of Fame: 1990

FURTHER READING

BOOKS

Ayer, Eleanor H. *Margaret Bourke-White: Photographing the World,* 1992 (juvenile)
Bourke-White, Margaret. *Portrait of Myself,* 1963
Daffron, Carolyn. *Margaret Bourke-White,* 1988 (juvenile)
Encyclopedia Americana, 1995
Encyclopedia Britannica, 1995
Goldberg, Vicki. *Margaret Bourke-White: A Biography,* 1986
Siegel, Beatrice. *An Eye on the World: Margaret Bourke-White, Photographer,* 1980 (juvenile)

Silverman, Jonathan. *For the World to See: The Life of Margaret Bourke-White*, 1983
Who Was Who, Vol. V
World Book Encyclopedia, 1996

PERIODICALS

American Heritage, Oct./Nov. 1986, p.10
Current Biography Yearbook 1940; 1971 (obituary)
New York Times, Aug. 28, 1971, p.1; Apr. 3, 1988, Section 2, p.37
Newsweek, Sep. 6, 1971, p.75
People, Sep. 8, 1986, p.10; Apr. 25, 1988, p.31
Time, Sep. 6, 1971, p.46

OBITUARY

Alexander Calder   1898-1976
American Sculptor and Artist
Creator of the Mobile Art Form

BIRTH

Alexander Calder was born on July 22, 1898, in Lawnton, Pennsylvania, a small town that later became part of Philadelphia. His parents were the prominent sculptor Alexander Stirling Calder and portrait painter Nanette (Lederer) Calder. His father was best known for *The Fountain of Energy,* installed at the San Francisco International Exposition in 1915. His grandfather, Alexander Milne Calder, was also a sculptor, noted for his colossal statue of William Penn erected at Philadelphia's City Hall in 1894. Young Alexander was nicknamed "Sandy" as a boy and was called by that name throughout his life by close friends and family. He had a sister, Peggy, who was born two years before him in Paris, France.

YOUTH

The Calders moved around quite often during Sandy's childhood. In 1906, his father came down with tuberculosis, and the family moved from Pennsylvania to a health ranch in Gracie, Arizona, for him to rest and recuperate. The following year, they settled in Pasadena, California. Calder remembers these years as hectic, but happy. In Arizona, he occasionally rode on a horse or donkey, met some Apaches, and saw cowboys rounding up and branding cattle. He also enjoyed making little playthings and odds and ends, such as a miniature castle for his sister's doll and a toy cannon that shot caps, made from an empty rifle cartridge. While in Pasadena, Calder was allowed to use some space in the cellar as a workshop, where he worked at twisting and cutting bits of wire, wood, tin, cork, and other materials into little movable animals and things. His schoolmates and friends liked coming to hang around the workshop to watch and take part. Calder's Uncle Ron, who was himself a whiz at building things, encouraged him to keep at it.

In 1910 the family moved back east to Croton-on-Hudson, about 40 miles north of New York City. Life in Croton-on-Hudson was also very agreeable. Calder's father's health had improved and he was working again on his sculpture. He was glad to be back near New York City, which was regarded as the center of the American art world. The family lived in the "Old Gate House" on the grounds of a large estate overlooking the Hudson River. Calder's mother had a studio to paint in, and Calder once again had a workshop in the cellar where he tinkered around trying to get little mechanical trains to run on wooden rails. He liked riding his bike around Croton. In the winter he could ice-skate on an artificial pond near the house, or on snowy days ride with his friend on a sled right into the center of town. Being the new boy in town did land him into some fights, but Calder remembers holding his own, and he eventually made lots of friends. The house was filled with visitors from all walks of life. One of them, the painter Everett Shinn, took a good deal of interest in Calder's mechanical projects.

Calder's father then rented a work studio in Manhattan, in New York City, and the family moved once again, this time to Spuyten Duyvil, closer to New York City. In 1913, just as Calder (now in high school) and his sister were getting used to life there, their father was appointed "acting head of sculpture" for the upcoming San Francisco Fair of 1915. The family picked up and headed west once more, renting houses first in San Francisco and then across the bay in Berkeley, where Peggy started college. Calder had his usual workshop in all these places and was intrigued by the machinery and brightly colored decorations of the cable cars in San Francisco. By now, he was close to finishing high school and was thinking about going to college, but he had not decided on a career.

EDUCATION

Calder remembers crying on the first day he started school at age six in Philadelphia. He later attended the McKinley School in Pasadena and Croton Public School in New York. He started secondary school at Yonkers High School in New York, and completed it at Lowell High School in Berkeley. Calder graduated from Lowell in 1915.

Although he had been surrounded by painting and sculpture throughout his youth, Calder had no thoughts of becoming an artist. Instead, his interest in mechanical gadgets and tinkering in his workshop led him to decide to study engineering. In 1915, he entered Stevens Institute of Technology in Hoboken, New Jersey. There, Calder proved to be a good student, especially in math, while still going to parties and dances and finding time to play on the lacrosse team. He received a degree in mechanical engineering from Stevens Institute in 1919. "Finally," he later wrote in his memoir *Calder: An Autobiography with Pictures*, "came the big day of graduation, and next the getting of a job."

FIRST JOBS

For the next several years, Calder worked at a variety of engineering and drafting jobs in New Jersey, New York, Missouri, Ohio, and West Virginia, most of which he found dull and routine. Looking for a change, he signed on as a seaman aboard a freighter sailing from New York to San Francisco in 1922. Once out west, he worked for a while in a logging camp in Washington state.

Around this time, he began to draw and paint a little. Tired of simply working at odd jobs, he returned to New York in 1923 and began to study drawing and painting in earnest at the Art Students League in New York City. He particularly enjoyed his classes with John Sloan and George Luks, two well-known American artists and teachers, because they did not tell students what to do, but instead helped them to find their own way.

Calder developed a knack for doing quick sketches in one line, which led to his first paid art job. He drew half-page layouts for the *Police Gazette* covering horse shows, boxing matches, the Barnum and Bailey Circus, Coney Island, and so forth, for which he received $20 apiece. During his three years at art school, he sometimes lived with his parents, who were back in New York, and sometimes in various cheap, rented rooms. Calder liked the circus so much that he kept going back and did a couple of weeks' worth of drawings that were published as a small book in 1926 called *Animal Sketching*. The next year, after holding an exhibition of his paintings at the Artists' Gallery in New York, he decided to set out on his own and go to Paris, where new and exciting developments in the world of modern art were taking place.

CAREER HIGHLIGHTS

THE CIRCUS

In the stimulating atmosphere of Paris, Calder's personality, talents, and training started to come together in his art. Basically, he was still a child at heart and liked to have fun. So, while seriously at work trying to make a living doing illustrations for American advertising agencies in Paris, or designing toys for a manufacturer located in Oshkosh, Wisconsin, he kept fooling around with scraps of wire and wood, just as he had done as a boy in his workshop. By 1927, Calder had put together a miniature circus, complete with clowns, acrobats, trapeze artists, and so on. Playing the part of announcer and ringmaster himself, he invited his newly found European and American friends to watch them perform. Deceptively and childishly simple, full of playful wit and humor, *Le Cirque Calder (Calder's Circus)* became all the rage in Paris. Many years later, in 1961, a short film was made of one such performance.

A NEW APPROACH TO SCULPTURE

Without losing his playful attitude, Calder combined his wire-twisting experience with his knack for single-line drawings. The result was a new kind of sculpture, made entirely of wire. Calder's first outstanding wire sculptures, done in 1926, were two standing figures of African-American dancer and singer Josephine Baker, who was extremely popular in Parisian nightclubs and music halls. These figures were followed over the next few years by many similar works, including studies of animals and portraits of people. His most elaborate wire sculpture is an almost-life-size group of acrobats called *The Brass Family*, made in 1929. It now can be seen in New York City's Whitney Museum of American Art. The originality of his works won the respect of many European experimental artists of the day. Fernand Leger, an abstract painter, declared Calder to be the most important living modern American artist. The international art world seemed to be deeply impressed by Calder's idea that art could be fun.

ART IN MOTION

Calder himself was especially influenced by the Dutch painter Piet Mondrian, whose abstract paintings of plain rectangular forms seemed to have an uncanny life of their own that was very different from the reality of everyday things. By 1930, Calder began to make abstract pieces in wire, bending it into curved and angular three-dimensional shapes and patterns. Some of these constructions looked like little solar systems, suggesting planetary movement in space. Then, in a leap of imagination that also drew on his love of animated toys, Calder hit on the idea of adding motion to his abstract sculptures. His first attempts in the early 1930s were given the French name "mobiles" (meaning movable or changeable) by his friend, French artist Marcel Duchamp. These first mobiles used hand cranks or little motors to make them move. Calder's father came to their exhibition in Paris and did not quite know what to say, but he did admire his son's mechanical ingenuity.

Calder himself was not completely satisfied with his new work. Because he found mechanical movement boring, stiff, and repetitive, he wanted something that would appear to move by itself in free and unpredictable ways, as if propelled by invisible forces, or by the very air itself. It was here that Calder's mathematical and engineering training in weight, balance, leverage, and opposing forces came into full play in his artwork. To get a light, airy, delicate feeling, Calder eventually suspended his mobiles from ceilings. The effect was astonishing; Calder had created both a new artistic medium and an innovative method of display. His was one of the truly original creations in the history of art.

His first large-scale installation was in 1939 when the Museum of Modern Art in New York commissioned a large mobile for its main stairwell. After that, Calder turned out mobiles in all sizes, shapes, and varied moods and attitudes. For example, the 4-by-3-foot mobile *Hanging Spider* (circa 1940) is abstract, although it does suggest a spider hanging from a web; while the giant hanging mobile *Ghost* (1964), measuring some 24 by 35 feet and amazingly complex and mysterious, is purely abstract. The great physicist Albert Einstein, who developed the theory of the relativity of time and space, is said to have spent three hours in silence looking at a Calder mobile, after which he said simply, "I wish I had thought of that."

ART AT REST

Calder was not content to stick to mobiles. Some of his sculptures didn't move, and when his sculptor friend Jean Arp said jokingly that these works now had to be called "stabiles," the name stuck. Like mobiles, Calder's stabiles varied greatly in size and mood, but all had the unmis-

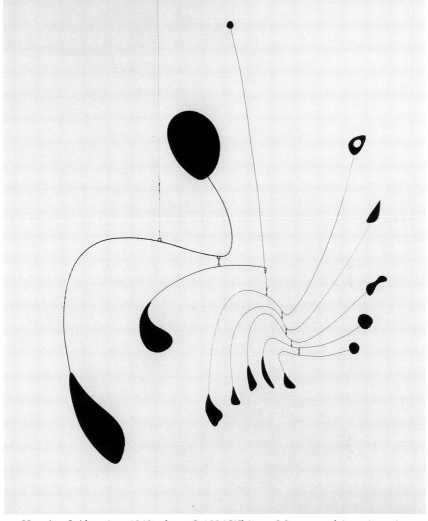

Hanging Spider, circa 1940; photo © 1996 Whitney Museum of American Art

takable Calder spirit of imagination and fun. Some of them stood on arched supports so that a viewer could actually walk underneath and through them, and they offered remarkably different perspectives when seen from different angles.

Over the years, as Calder was commissioned to do works for large cities and major institutions, he created a number of stabiles that were monumental in size. Among them are the 40-foot-high *La Grande Voile (Big Sail;* 1964) at the Massachusetts Institute of Technology, in Cambridge, Massachusetts, and the 50-foot-high *Stegosaurus* (1973) by the City Hall in Hartford, Connecticut. Calder went on to design and install his highly acclaimed monumental sculptures in public places the world over. He assembled most of his mobiles and smaller stabiles by himself, but he would design his massive works in small models and then give the tasks of casting, cutting, and assembling these great sections of metal to professional ironworkers and steel-plate foundries in the United States or overseas.

OTHER KINDS OF ART

While noted mainly for his mobiles and stabiles, Calder was a highly productive and remarkably versatile artist in many other media as well. One of his loves was jewelry, which he hammered out of gold, silver, brass, and copper into necklaces, headpieces, pins, and bracelets in a wide variety of designs. Calder also turned out paintings, wood carvings, sculptures in bronze, and tapestries. In addition, he illustrated a number of children's books, which won him recognition, and designed hundreds of prints and posters that became immensely popular all over the country. He even designed a race car for BMW. Perhaps Calder's most unusual project was a commission in 1973 from the airline Braniff International to paint one of its giant DC-8 passenger jets with one of his designs. Called *Flying Colors*, the plane made international flights for several years.

In October 1976, to honor his long career and the wide range of his works, a major retrospective exhibition called "Calder's Universe," which he attended, opened at the Whitney Museum of American Art. He died only a few weeks later, on November 11, 1976, at the age of 78.

LEGACY

Innovation, gaiety, wit, invention, technical competence, humor, joy — there are the lasting qualities of Calder's art, according to many in the art world who were quick to offer tributes after his death. William Rubin, director of painting and sculpture at the Museum of Modern Art, wrote that "Alexander Calder was the first American modernist working in any medium to impose himself on the history of art as an artist of worldwide importance, and to be universally recognized."

Thomas Hoving, director of the Metropolitan Museum of Art, said that "Calder must be considered a virtual giant of the last two generations of American art. Inventive, joyful, yet powerful, and at the same time imbued with an excellence of craftsmanship, his diverse works of art will surely last, bringing a sense of celebration and lively discussion for future generations."

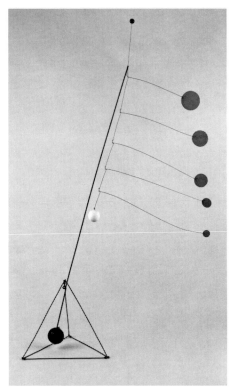

Calderberry Bush, 1932; photo © 1996
Whitney Museum of American Art

John Canaday, the former art critic for the *New York Times,* said that "His invention of the mobile opened a whole new era of 20th-century sculpture. No other artist I can think of combined so much wit with such unfailing aesthetic discipline. Everything he did, from the kitchen forks he improvised for use at home to a multi-ton public sculpture, bore his very personal stamp."

H. Harvard Arnason, an art historian who has written two books about Calder, wrote that "It wasn't just that he created sculpture that moved. The objects were beautiful in themselves. His stabiles were some of the great monuments of the 20th century. He had a lightness of touch but at the same time could achieve architectural monumentality."

Henry Berg, deputy director of the Guggenheim Museum, said this: "A genuine and original form-giver of the 20th century, he has literally populated the world with evidence of his unquenchable creative energy. To all those who have been touched by his genius, Calder's name is synonymous with the profound as well as the lighthearted in artistic expression. To his friends, the world is a much dimmer place today."

MARRIAGE AND FAMILY

Calder met Louisa James of Concord, Massachusetts, on shipboard in June 1929 during a return trip from Paris to the United States, and they were married in her hometown in January 1931. Thereafter, they divided their time between a farmhouse in Roxbury, Connecticut, and a home in Sache, France. Louisa, a distant relative of novelist Henry James and philosopher William James, shared her husband's interest in art, and the two enjoyed decorating their homes together. They had two children, Sandra and Mary, who loved to dance with their father as their mother played the accordion. When the girls grew up and married, Alexander and Louisa Calder soon had plenty of grandchildren to entertain.

Always a friendly host, Calder—usually in blue jeans and a red flannel shirt—liked to show people around his cluttered studio. He also enjoyed giving tours of his house, which was filled with everyday things made or decorated by him, including a toaster, tables, ashtrays, lamps, spoons and ladles, door latches, and even trash cans. An exhibit of 350 of these home-made household items, called "The Intimate World of Alexander Calder," was held in 1990 at the Cooper-Hewitt Museum in New York City.

SELECTED WORKS

WRITINGS

Calder: An Autobiography with Pictures, 1966

ILLUSTRATIONS

Calder, Alexander. *Animal Sketching,* 1926
Fables of Aesop/According to Sir Roger L'Estrange, 1931
Three Young Rats and Other Rhymes, 1944
Coleridge, Samuel. *The Rime of the Ancient Mariner,* 1946
La Fontaine, Jean de. *Selected Fables,* 1948
Wilbur, Richard, ed. *A Bestiary,* 1955

HONORS AND AWARDS

Venice Biennale: 1952, first prize
Carnegie Prize (Carnegie Museum of Art): 1958, first prize
Architectural League of New York: 1960, gold medal
Creative Arts Award (Brandeis University): 1962
Edward MacDowell Medal: 1963
Gold Medal (American Academy and Institute of Arts and Letters): 1971
Grand Prix (National des Arts et Lettres, France): 1974
United Nations Peace Medal: 1975
Presidential Medal of Freedom: 1977

FURTHER READING

BOOKS

Bourdon, David. *Calder: Mobilist/Ringmaster/Innovator,* 1980
Calder, Alexander. *Calder: An Autobiography with Pictures,* 1966
Contemporary Artists, 1996
Encyclopedia Americana, 1995
Encyclopedia Britannica, 1995
Kuh, Katharine. *The Artist's Voice,* 1960
Lipman, Jean. *Alexander Calder and His Magical Mobiles,* 1981 (juvenile)
Lipman, Jean. *Calder's Circus,* 1972
Lipman, Jean. *Calder's Universe,* 1976

Marchesseau, Daniel. *The Intimate World of Alexander Calder*, 1990
Mulas, Ugo, and H. H. Arnason. *Calder*, 1971
Rodman, Selden. *Conversations with Artists*, 1957
Who Was Who, Vol. VII
World Book Encyclopedia, 1996

PERIODICALS

ARTnews, Mar. 1992, p.150
Christian Science Monitor, Nov. 7, 1989, p.10; June 15, 1992, p.16
Current Biography Yearbook 1966; 1977 (obituary)
New York Times, Nov. 12, 1976, p.A1; Oct. 22, 1989, Section 2, p.1
Time, Nov. 22, 1976, p.63
Washington Times, Jan. 2, 1990, p.E1

OBITUARY

Mark Chagall   1887-1985
Russian Artist
Painter and Stained-Glass Artist Acclaimed
for His Imaginative Style

BIRTH

Marc Chagall (pronounced sha-GALL) was born Moyshe
Shagal on July 7, 1887, in Vitebsk, a small town in Russia
near the Polish border. Marc was one of ten children of
Zakhar and Ida Tchernine Chagall. The Russian language
uses a different alphabet, known as Cyrillic, and Chagall's
name is sometimes translated as Shagall.

YOUTH

Chagall and his family were Hasidic Jews at a time when anti-Semitism was very prevalent throughout Russia and much of Europe. Jewish people routinely faced discrimination, and worse. They were forced to live in certain areas and were forbidden from moving without government permission. In Russia, Jews were not allowed to be full citizens.

But Chagall and his family lived in a close-knit, orderly Jewish community. Like their neighbors, they were members of the mystical and devout Jewish sect known as Hasidim. Hasidic Jews followed very strict customs. Men wore large dark hats and dark clothing, while women stayed mostly at home tending to their children. Religious and dietary laws were closely observed. The Hasidim believed in the mercy of God and the joyous expression of religious feeling through music and dance. Chagall and his family believed that God exists everywhere, and in everything: "He comes down and dwells among the downtrodden. Thus all, animals and humans, are invested with a heavenly spirit." They had a saying that "Behind every blade of grass stands an angel urging it on: Grow! Grow!"

Marc's community and family influenced his entire life as an artist. One grandfather was a rabbi; the other was a butcher who the family once found up on the roof of the house munching on raw carrots. When company came, his uncle liked to play his fiddle, even though he played "like a cobbler." Marc's father was a poor laborer who worked in a herring warehouse, while his mother earned a little money running a small neighborhood grocery. Years later, Chagall would incorporate images based on these and other family members, as well as other experiences from his childhood, into his work.

Chagall's parents strongly promoted the importance of religion and education. But like most children, Chagall was more interested in recreation. His idea of a fun afternoon was swimming in the Dvina River or watching a bonfire from his cottage roof. His parents had other plans for him, though. They engaged a rabbi to teach him religious ways and sent him to the town school. But Chagall was too restless. Sometimes he skipped his religious lessons, and while at school he was good only at geometry. When he was called upon to stand up to participate in other subjects, he suddenly developed a stammer and sat down.

It soon became clear that Chagall was not well-suited to formal education. Nonetheless, the young man learned a great deal about life by observing the special ways of his hometown. In his mind, he filed away images of his brothers and sisters, his parents and grandparents, his neighbors, and their cattle and cottages. Young Chagall added something extra to his storehouse of memories: a child's fantasy. He would imagine that the world was inhabited by flying people, flying animals, flying flowers, and flying lovers. Pretty girls with wings soared overhead. Couples floated through the twilight, arm in arm. Jewish and Christian symbols were everywhere. Birds and fish played violins and flutes. And the colors! Cows were blue, people were red, horses were green. As a child, Chagall stored many memories of his Vitebsk fantasy land. "It was from this milieu," wrote John Russell in the *New York Times*, "at once isolated and immensely alive, that Marc Chagall drew not only his awareness of the injustices and inequalities of human life but a vast repertory of symbol and allusion, ritual and wry humor, aspiration and irrepressible feeling. By the time [he became an art student] he had the subject matter of a lifetime at his fingers' ends, and he was to be sustained by it throughout the next eight decades."

Chagall himself wrote, "From the moment I was born in my hometown, when I saw this land, this sky and my parents running around earning their meager living, I felt that the story of color is the story of life itself."

EARLY MEMORIES

In Vitebsk, most men grew up to be laborers or merchants, but neither prospect excited Marc Chagall. He dreamed of being a singer, dancer, or poet. His mother and father were sympathetic, but the closest they could offer was to get him a job learning the trade of a neighborhood photographer. Chagall's assignment was to improve older people's portraits by painting out the wrinkles. It was boring work, but one day, when a schoolmate observed that he did it rather well, Chagall agreed. At that point he made a big decision. "One fine day . . . as my mother was putting the bread in the oven, I went up to her, and taking her flour-smeared elbow, I said to her, 'Mama . . . I want to be a painter'." Soon, he was off to art school.

EDUCATION

Chagall showed little promise in art school. In fact, he went to four schools without achieving any great distinction. He decided to venture to the Russian capital, St. Petersburg. At that time, Russia was ruled by an autocratic government headed up by the czar, an all-powerful hereditary ruler similar to an emperor. Under the czarist regime, Jews could not leave a town unless they had a job elsewhere. So, in 1907, Chagall persuaded a merchant from Vitebsk to hire him as his representative in St. Petersburg.

It was a tough year for Chagall in St. Petersburg. After he failed the entrance exam to the best school in the city, he settled for a school of lower reputation. Unsatisfied, he then studied a few months with the noted artist Leon Bakst, but this did not work out either. He also failed at several different jobs. Unable to afford an apartment, he slept wherever he could rent a bed. Once, he was jailed because his residence papers were not in order. In a St. Petersburg prison, he got better food and rest than he did on his own. Despite his setbacks, Chagall was still certain that his future was tied to his art. He saw potential in designing sets for the theater and studied theater design with several notables of the Russian theater. Attending a lecture on drama, he met a young woman named Bella Rosenfeld. It was love at first sight, and they later married.

CAREER HIGHLIGHTS

Eager to pursue a serious art career, Chagall returned to Vitebsk determined to find a rich patron, someone who would be willing to support his career financially. He found one in Max Vinaver, a prosperous merchant. In 1910, Vinaver paid for Chagall to travel to Paris, France, to paint. Paris, in 1910, was the center of the art world. Many artists were drawn to Paris, which became the birthplace of modern art.

For Chagall, it was a remarkable visit. Suddenly in the right place at the right time, he met with nearly instant success. The young man from the Russian countryside was almost immediately sharing the artistic community of Paris with such artists as Pablo Picasso, Henri Matisse, Theodore Rousseau, Amedeo Modigliani, and Diego Rivera. Chagall found the work of the young French painter Robert Delaunay particularly influential. Delaunay was involved in the schools of painting known as fauvism and orphism, which relied on color to show shape and depth. Many believe this partly explains Chagall's purple cows and red women.

Critics liked Chagall's early works, and so did the public. He was especially admired for combining his memories of village life in Vitebsk, including the houses, farms, social events, and animals, with a new style that seemed a precursor to surrealism. A movement that dominated French painting and literature in the 1920s and 1930s, surrealism stressed the importance of imagination and dream states, coupled with insight into the subject matter. In Chagall's paintings, these qualities often led to the use of fantasy images. From cubism he borrowed its geometric shapes but gave them his own fantasy renderings. Combining his vivid imagination with new painting styles, Chagall's early paintings struck the viewer with their joyous style, vibrant colors, whimsical moods, and unusual and fantastic images, particularly his depictions of humans, animals, and angels floating in the sky. Within a year, Chagall put the finishing touches on I and the Village (also translated as Me and the Village), a masterwork that years later would be exhibited in New York City's Museum of Modern Art. Another noted painting from this early period was Paris Through My Window (1913), dominated by the Eiffel Tower and streaked with light but also with images of modern technology such as an upside-down train and a person parachuting. "I don't understand them at all," Chagall himself once said about his paintings; "they are not literature. They are only pictorial arrangements of images that obsess me."

Soon Chagall found himself befriended and influenced by Guillaume Apollinaire, the foremost French poet of the day. It was Apollinaire who coined the term "surrealism" to describe the daring and fantastic art that Chagall and other artists were creating in Paris. The Italian-born Apollinaire was intrigued with this young Russian and his strikingly original work. He introduced Chagall to the most important art dealer in Berlin, Germany, and soon Chagall became quite a success. By 1914, at the age of 27, Chagall had painted many of his best-known works and had exhibited in Paris, Berlin, and Moscow. Only a few years after arriving as an unknown student from St. Petersburg, Chagall emerged as a major figure in the international art world.

Many different types of artists worked in Paris at that time, and many different artistic movements got their start there. Chagall was influenced by them all. But throughout, he remained true to his own artistic vision, as Robert Wernick explained in *Smithsonian* magazine: "Paris was full of schools, movements: every year brought its own new ism. Chagall was in the thick of it all. He borrowed ideas right and left, but he never gave up his independence, he would belong to no group. He could flatten out his shapes like the Cubists, he could give free rein to color like the Fauves, he could twist his figures painfully like the Expressionists, he could bathe incongruous figures in a dreamlike atmosphere long before anyone had thought of the word Surrealism. But he always remained his own man, distrustful of theories and rigid categories. He was willing to fill his work with symbols, but he had little use for people putting labels on them. 'I have slept very well without Freud,' he said."

WORLD WAR I

After achieving fame and fortune in Paris, Chagall bought a round-trip ticket to Vitebsk in 1914, intending to marry his fiancee, Bella Rosenfeld, and return with her to Paris. They married in 1915, but the outbreak of World War I the previous fall made it impossible for them to leave Russia.

In 1917, Russia was engulfed by the Russian Revolution, the beginning of a civil war that overthrew the czarist government and ultimately resulted in the development of the Communist system and the creation of the Union of Soviet Socialist Republics (USSR). At first, Chagall welcomed it. For one thing, it made him, as a Jew, a full citizen, something the former government had outlawed. Second, it gave him full status as an artist. In fact, Chagall was appointed "Commissar for Art in Vitebsk." He was given the odd (and quite unsuccessful) mission of turning every villager into an artist. Chagall also found himself arguing with other Russian artists, who may have resented his success.

STARTING OVER

But by 1922, Chagall decided that Russia no longer had anything to offer him. Famous but penniless, he returned to Paris. His artworks had been sold or had disappeared in the war. Yet he was welcomed as a hero by the Surrealists and soon found work. His first commission was to illustrate the novel *Dead Souls* by noted Russian writer Nikolai Gogol. Chagall had to learn etching, a technique of drawing on metal plates for printing, and caught on fast. His fanciful illustrations were a success, soon leading to a second commission, for the *Fables of La Fontaine*, and then a third, to illustrate the Bible, for which he did 105 illustrations. His etchings and lithographs demanded more precision than his paintings, but Chagall met the requirement of these new mediums without losing the imaginative qualities in his art. He also continued to paint, producing such works as *Over Vitebsk* (1928) and *The Circus* (1931). Chagall traveled widely but kept his headquarters in Paris through the 1930s.

WORLD WAR II

By the late 1930s, with the German Nazi Army on the march, it became dangerous for Jews throughout Europe. In 1941, the Chagalls fled their adopted homeland as the German armies conquered France. They were very fortunate to find safe passage to the United States, moving to New York City. Marc called New York "this Babylon," referring to the ancient Biblical city known for its lack of morals. Chagall did create several important works in the United States, including *The Juggler* (1943) and *Cockcrow* (1944). With Leonide Massine, a dance choreographer and fellow Russian, he created the costumes and designed the sets for Igor Stravinsky's ballet *The Firebird* and for *Aleko*, based on a poem by Aleksandr Pushkin. The sets were beautiful and compelling to look at — even more so, perhaps, than the dancers. In fact, critic John Martin commented about the sets for *Aleko* that "so exciting are they in their own right that more than once one wished all those people would quit getting in front of them." Some of Chagall's other artworks of this period are said to have revealed his pessimism of a world at war.

WORLDWIDE RECOGNITION

After World War II, at age 60, Chagall neared the peak of his fame and creative powers. His works were commissioned all over the world, and he expanded into other types of art. In addition to painting, he also created works in stained glass, ceramics, and tapestry. There were exhibitions in many countries, and Chagall became a global celebrity.

The Fiddler, 1963

In France, he painted a new ceiling for the Paris Opera. He did stained-glass windows for the church at Assy and the cathedral at Metz. He created costumes and sets for the Paris Opera production of *Daphnis et Chloe.* In Israel, he designed a dozen windows representing the 12 tribes of Israel for a synagogue at the Hadassah Hebrew University Medical

Center. He also designed three huge tapestries on Old Testament themes for the Knesset, the Israeli parliament. On his 86th birthday, Chagall was honored by the French government, which created the National Museum of the Marc Chagall Biblical Message in Nice to exhibit his series of 62 paintings called *The Biblical Message.*

In the United States, Chagall's work includes the huge murals at the Metropolitan Opera in Lincoln Center in New York City. He also created stained-glass windows at the United Nations headquarters in New York City and the Union Church in Tarrytown, New York, as well as the *Four Seasons* mosaic at the First National Bank in Chicago.

Chagall lived to the age of 97. He died at his country villa in St. Paul de Vence, France, on March 28, 1985. Two years later, Chagall's art was once again displayed in the USSR, the politically unfriendly homeland he had turned his back on so many years before. With *glasnost,* the new policy of openness creating new opportunities for the exchange of political, intellectual, and artistic ideas, Chagall's works were exhibited at Moscow's Pushkin Museum. Critics called it the return of the native, and visitors stood in line for hours to see what had been hidden for decades in the storerooms of Russian museums.

LEGACY

Marc Chagall was one of the original pioneers of modern art and one of the most popular artists of modern times. He is considered a poetic visionary, celebrated for his vibrant colors and rich visual imagery. His greatest works combine both deep personal meaning and universal appeal. Unlike his many contemporaries who focused on techniques, Chagall celebrated the depth of human feelings, especially love and joy. "Chagall must have an angel in his head," Picasso once said.

Chagall's paintings can be found in art museums throughout the world. His stained-glass windows adorn churches and synagogues. He created opera and ballet stage sets and costumes, book illustrations, ceramics, murals, watercolors, pastels. He once said "I work in whatever medium likes me at the moment." Regardless of the medium, Chagall employed an individual style that was colorful, joyous, and magical. It was part folk art with its themes of ordinary life; part surrealism, with its fanciful treatments; and part a reflection of the basic contentment of a successful talent. Some critics called it "naive"; others scorned it as "Jewish Disneyland." But Chagall was convinced that his style was the right one. As he said of Picasso and the cubists, whose paintings include fragmented and abstract shapes, "Let them eat their fill of their square pears on their triangular tables."

Chagall believed in his work and claimed that it would outlive him and his critics. "If I create with my heart, almost all my intentions remain," he once said. "If it is with my head, almost nothing. An artist must not fear to be himself, to express only himself. If he is absolutely and entirely sincere, what he says and does will be acceptable to others."

Despite the attacks of some critics, the public loved his work. "[Chagall] had an enormous constituency," according to John Russell, "one that overran all boundaries of age, creed, social status, or place of origin. Though he was not without his detractors, Chagall's sense of fantasy, his habitually gorgeous color, and gift for an immediately accessible poignancy won admirers wherever his work was shown.

"His unconventional world was a brightly colored melange of animals, flowers, people, embracing lovers, birds and fish playing musical instruments, nymphs, satyrs, winged female figures, Jewish and Christian symbols, vignettes of clustered roofs, and violins with angel's wings. These objects rarely if ever bore their natural hues: cows were likely to be blue, horses green, people red.

"This fantasy universe, sometimes poignantly sad but more often laughingly joyous, was childlike in it apparent simpleness yet strangely sophisticated in its perceptiveness. It was, moreover, a world without gravity, in which objects appeared to float in disparate juxtaposition while achieving a remarkable total harmony and rhythm."

MARRIAGE AND FAMILY

Marc Chagall married Bella Rosenfeld in Russia in 1915, amid the madness of World War I. Their daughter, Ida, was born the following year. During World War II, the Chagalls, having escaped Europe, settled into an apartment off Fifth Avenue in New York City, but never felt at home. In 1944, Chagall was crushed by the death of his wife, refusing to paint for nine months. Said the grieving Chagall: "All dressed in white or all in black, she has long floated across my canvases, guiding my art. I finish neither painting nor engraving without asking her 'yes or no'." Two years after the war, in 1947, he returned to Paris for good. Soon he met and married Valentine Brodsky, a divorced Russian. He nicknamed her "Clutter Vava" because she tried (unsuccessfully) to remove the clutter from his life.

Chagall always thrived on clutter and never permitted anyone to straighten out his studio. Within it were canvases, messy palettes, art books, photos of friends and relatives, and, in the corner, a phonograph usually playing Russian classical records. As his fame grew, so did his wealth. Chagall had a house on the elegant Ile St. Louis in Paris and kept a country estate at St. Paul de Vence in the south of France.

WRITINGS

My Life, 1960

HONORS AND AWARDS

Carnegie Prize (Carnegie Museum of Art): 1939
Erasmus Prize (Netherlands): 1960
Grand Cross of the Legion of Honor (France): 1977
Wolf Foundation Prize (Israel): 1981

FURTHER READING

BOOKS

Bober, Natalie. *Marc Chagall: Painter of Dreams*, 1991 (juvenile)
Chagall, Marc. *My Life*, 1960
Contemporary Artists, 1996
Encyclopedia Americana, 1995
Encyclopedia Britannica, 1995
Erben, Walter. *Marc Chagall*, 1957
Greenfeld, Howard. *Marc Chagall: An Introduction*, 1980 (juvenile)
Raboff, Ernest Lloyd. *Marc Chagall*, 1987 (juvenile)
Sweeney, J. J. *Marc Chagall*, 1946
Who Was Who, Vol. VIII
World Book Encyclopedia, 1996

PERIODICALS

ARTnews, Summer 1985, p.99
Current Biography Yearbook 1960; 1985 (obituary)
Harper's Bazaar, May 1985, p.174
Horizon, May 1985, p.49
New York Times, Mar. 29, 1985, p.A1; Sep. 13, 1987, Section 2, p.47; Mar. 29, 1996, p.B1
Newsweek, Apr. 8, 1985, p.78
Readers Digest, June 1987, p.180
Smithsonian, May 1985, p.66
Time, Apr. 8, 1985, p.85
U. S. News & World Report, Sep. 14, 1987, p.12

Helen Frankenthaler 1928-
American Artist
Abstract Painter and Creator of "Soak-Stain" Art

BIRTH

Helen Frankenthaler was born on December 12, 1928, in New York City. Her father was Alfred Frankenthaler, a New York Supreme Court justice, and her mother was Martha (Lowenstein) Frankenthaler, originally from Germany. The youngest of three girls, Helen has two sisters, Marjorie and Gloria.

YOUTH

Helen's childhood was near-perfect for her first ten years. She had every advantage that growing up in a wealthy family in one of the most exciting cities in the world could provide. Plus, she was adored by her father, who had told Helen that from the day she was born, there was something "special" about her. He nurtured her interest in art and richly rewarded it. When Helen was nine years old and had received honorable mention in a drawing contest, he took her to an exclusive jewelry store and bought her a 14-karat gold palette for her charm bracelet. When she was 11, her beloved father died of cancer. Helen recalled, "After he died, I was very depressed, but of course a child of 11 doesn't know she's depressed. She just feels terrible and frightened and alone."

EDUCATION

Helen attended two of the best private schools in New York City, first the Brearley School and then, to prepare for college, the Dalton School. It was while she was a student at Dalton that Frankenthaler began visiting the many art museums and galleries in New York. She also took ballet lessons and studied French. She attended Bennington College in Vermont, where she studied art. She graduated from Bennington in 1949 with a bachelor of arts degree.

Several of her college teachers helped her decide to become an artist. She was very interested in writing, and even served as editor of the college newspaper while at Bennington. Yet two of her teachers redirected that interest. Her art teacher at Dalton was a famous Mexican artist, Rufino Tamayo, who was the first to inspire in Frankenthaler a serious interest in painting. At Bennington, the "cubist" painter Paul Feeley became her teacher and friend. Cubism was a school of painting from the early 20th century that emphasized fragmented geometric forms juxtaposed in surprising ways. These two men contributed greatly to Helen's choice of art as her career.

MAJOR INFLUENCES

When Frankenthaler was 22 years old, she met renowned art critic Clement Greenberg, who had helped establish the career of painter Jackson Pollock. Frankenthaler and Greenberg had a five-year romance that catapulted her into the most influential art circles in New York. They visited all the art galleries in the city together, then they traveled across Europe to study the great masters and the new painters. Not only did these experiences help Frankenthaler grow in her understanding of painting, but Greenberg introduced her to some of the leading abstract expressionists, including Pollock and Willem and Elaine de Kooning.

Abstract expressionism was an art movement that originated in New York City in the 1940s. It may have been inspired by Hans Hofmann (who was later one of Frankenthaler's teachers) and Arshile Gorky, both immigrants to the United States. Hofmann was experimenting with using blobs of paint to create abstract designs on canvas, while Gorky was using bold strokes of color. Abstract expressionism was a school of art, a description of the work of particular artists who were rebelling against old forms of "literal" or landscape art and creating abstract, non-realistic images instead. The more famous artists associated with abstract expressionism were Pollock, who had mastered the drip-and-splash look on canvas; Willem de Kooning, who drew extraordinarily shaped fig-ures; Franz Kline, whose work was a sort of calligraphy (an elegant let-tering or line-drawing style); and Robert Motherwell (later Franken-thaler's husband), who was known for creating a more peaceful but ab-stract effect. In the past, what was happening in art in the great cities of Europe would affect the rest of the world. For the first time, what was happening in the art circles in America in the 1940s greatly impacted the art that would emerge from Europe in the 1950s. It trumpeted the inde-pendence of American art.

Abstract expressionism had a huge impact on Frankenthaler. In fact, an abstract exhibit by Pollock inspired her to create her own style. When she first saw Pollock's "drip" paintings covering an entire wall, she said, "It was original, and it was beautiful, and it was new, and it was saying the most that could be said in painting up to that point—and it really drew me in." Her reaction to this show resulted in her creation of *Mountains and Sea* (1952), which some consider to be her greatest contribution to the color movement in abstract expressionism.

CAREER HIGHLIGHTS

"SOAK-STAIN" TECHNIQUE

Frankenthaler's main contribution to modern art was the soak-stain tech-nique, a new way to paint that she created when she was only in her 20s. She had just returned to her studio in New York from a trip to Nova Scotia, an island off the northeastern coast of Canada. Inspired by Pollock's style, she thinned her oil paints so they would flow like water and then poured them onto her canvas, allowing the texture and weave of the canvas to pull the paint into it. This technique was later called "soak-stain." Frankenthaler became famous with her first work created in this manner, *Mountains and Sea*, an abstract expression of blues, greens, and pinks representing the landscape of Nova Scotia, which she completed in a single day. It was this bold, original expression that pro-vided the shift from abstract expressionism to the "color-field" painting of the 1960s. In this new style, color could be captured on canvas without the heaviness and thickness of the medium of oil paint.

Nature Abhors a Vacuum, 1973

Unlike many artists, Frankenthaler became famous at an early age, and fortune soon followed. She worked hard for her fame and demanded much from herself. She has claimed to throw away a dozen paintings for every one she keeps. Her primary objective has always been to "make a beautiful picture," an aim unique in a generation of artists whose dominant theme in painting was the anger and gloom of modern life. Her paintings, capturing softness, gentleness, and serenity, have been criticized for these qualities. Some critics have compared her works to "wet paint rags," and others have considered her work simply overrated. As Deborah Solomon wrote in the *New York Times Magazine,* "Her paintings . . . seem intent on providing worldly pleasure—and this is both their strength and their weakness. Her best paintings are lushly beautiful. Her lesser paintings are too beautiful; they fit in a bit too comfortably with the decor. If her work dazzles us with its unabashed loveliness, it also makes us ask, is it enough for a painting to be lovely to look at?"

Frankenthaler's paintings fill the canvas, sometimes with vivid combinations of bold colors, as in *Buddha's Court* (1964), *Tangerine* (1964), and

Nature Abhors a Vacuum (1973). Other times, the colors are pastel and less vibrant, as in *The Bay* (1963) and *Hint from Bassano* (1973). Yet, there is more to Frankenthaler's paintings than random colors. The arrangement of her colors are the result of thoughtful expression, and they are a balancing act. "Color," she has said, "doesn't work unless it works in space. Color alone is just decoration—you might as well be making a shower curtain." Frankenthaler describes her paintings as the interaction between her feelings and artistic order, although she does not start out with a particular thought in mind. Her rules for painting, if they can be called that, are "Think, feel, worry, approach, ACT! Then stand back and look. Edit things that don't come off." She uses her body motion to paint, called "action painting"—getting into the movement of the colors—and she is continuously moving the canvas around the room for different perspectives.

With abstract art, there is always the human urge to identify some recognizable form. Many of Frankenthaler's paintings suggest the landscape or subject matter for which they are named. Her *Swan Lake* series is an example of this. She once explained, "When I was young there was a magazine I loved called *Child Life*. Each edition had a game . . . in which there were hidden yet definable images within the obvious images. For example, if you saw a landscape with trees, you could decipher a rabbit hidden in the leaves of a tree . . . . Looking back, the 'swans' in *Swan Lake I* (1961) remind me of that experience. . . . I started with blue, and . . . at some point I recognized the birdlike shape—I was ready for it—and I developed it from there."

Much of Frankenthaler's work, though, is too abstract to be recognized as actual beings or things in the real world, although almost all of her earlier work was inspired by a geographic location or the "feel" of the ocean or a season. But once she is inspired, it is the use of colors that shapes the painting. Frankenthaler acknowledges that many people like to see more conventional themes in her work than she had intended. Her own interpretation of her art is quite simple: "Anything that has beauty . . . gives pleasure—a sense of rightness, as in being one with nature."

AN ABSTRACT EXPRESSIONIST IN TODAY'S ART WORLD

In her recent works, Frankenthaler has continued to use color with more intensity than before, especially when she has worked with painting on paper. Yet these works have failed to earn the acclaim of her earlier art and to inspire today's changing forms of painting. Frankenthaler has continued to be a model abstract expressionist while the rest of the art world has moved on. Today, her work stands apart from most contemporary art. Many critics consider much of her work dated because she has not changed with the times. One critic called her recent paintings "Soapsuds and whitewash!" Another was more generous in describing this work as "romantically deft." Her work continues to earn sharply divided reviews, both glowing and disparaging.

But Frankenthaler is not bothered by the negative reviews. She is secure that the essence of her paintings and the feelings they generate in the viewer will continue to "advance truth, beauty, and pleasure." When asked recently to respond to critics who say that her work is too beautiful, Frankenthaler had this to say: "I think people are threatened by the word beauty today. In some circles the word implies schmaltzy and passé. But the darkest Rembrandts and Goyas, the most somber music of Beethoven, the most tragic poems by Eliot are all full of light and beauty. Great, moving art that speaks the truth is beautiful art."

To this day, Frankenthaler's works continue to be widely exhibited. During the 1980s, her work was shown in major cities all over the world. In 1985, she had an exhibit at New York's Guggenheim Museum of 70 of her paintings on paper, an effect different from that created by her painting on canvas, where the texture of the canvas adds to the complete visual experience. She continues to have periodic shows at the Emmerich Gallery in New York City.

In 1989, a huge retrospective of her work opened at the Museum of Modern Art in New York before traveling to other major American cities. While most retrospectives of living artists seem to represent the completion of one's life work, Frankenthaler did not feel that way. "I don't think a retrospective is a finality, it's a summing up, an opportunity to see where you have been and where you will go from there." For the 1989 retrospective, she wanted the public to see that "in my art I've moved and have been able to grow. I've been someplace. Hopefully, others should be similarly moved."

Frankenthaler feels that today there are not many people to whom she can relate or "artists whose work I want to see. It makes for a kind of loneliness." Hanging in her studio is a famous line from poet Marianne Moore: "The best cure for loneliness is solitude."

MARRIAGE AND FAMILY

Frankenthaler was married in 1958 to Robert Motherwell, a major abstract expressionist painter. They spent their honeymoon of several months in France and in Spain, where they painted and studied the French Basque and Spanish styles. When they returned to New York City, they renovated their 100-year-old brownstone building to capture the look of a Spanish villa, with pure white walls, ceilings the color of the

Mediterranean Sea, floors featuring parquet (multicolored woods) or Spanish tiles, and natural wood doors. Frankenthaler and Motherwell were married for 13 years before divorcing in 1971. Since then, Frankenthaler has lived and worked in New York City and Connecticut.

HONORS AND AWARDS

Paris Biennale (Paris Museum of Modern Art): 1959, first prize
Joseph E. Temple Gold Medal (Pennsylvania Academy of Fine Arts): 1968
Spirit of Achievement Award (Albert Einstein School of Medicine, New York): 1970
Garrett Award (Art Institute of Chicago): 1972
American Academy and Institute of Arts and Letters: 1974
Extraordinary Woman of Achievement (National Conference of Christians and Jews): 1978
National Council on the Arts (National Endowment of the Arts): 1985
New York City Mayor's Award of Honor for Art and Culture: 1986

FURTHER READING

BOOKS

Carmean, E. A., Jr. *Helen Frankenthaler: A Paintings Retrospective,* 1989
Contemporary Artists, 1996
Encyclopedia Americana, 1995
Encyclopedia Britannica, 1995
Who's Who in America, 1996
Who's Who in American Art, 1995-96
World Book Encyclopedia, 1996

PERIODICALS

ARTNews, Summer 1985, p.79
Current Biography Yearbook 1966
Los Angeles Times, Feb. 8, 1990, p.F1
New York Times Magazine, May 14, 1989, p.30
New Yorker, Dec. 23, 1985, p.64
Newsweek, June 12, 1989, p.62
People, Dec. 4, 1989, p.117
Time, June 12, 1989, p.74

ADDRESS

Andre Emmerich Gallery
41 East 57th Street
New York, NY 10022

Jasper Johns 1930-
American Artist
Pioneering Pop-Art Painter

BIRTH

Jasper Johns, Jr., was born in Augusta, Georgia, on May 15, 1930, the only child of Jasper Johns, Sr., and Jean (Riley) Johns. Jasper calls his father a "ne'er-do-well" farmer; his parents separated soon after his birth.

YOUTH

Johns had an unhappy childhood. When his mother and father split up, neither wanted to keep him. He went to live with his grandparents in Allentown, South Carolina. After

63

his grandfather died while Jasper was in third grade, the boy was passed from relative to relative, sometimes living with his mother and stepfather, sometimes with other relatives. He settled in with his Aunt Gladys for six years. She taught school in a small rural South Carolina town without telephones or electricity. Johns once said that when he was a little boy, he had no idea what the rest of the world was like.

Johns was a very shy child who kept to himself. Although he was the schoolteacher's nephew, few people paid him much attention. But the one thing people did notice on occasion was that he was good at drawing pictures. As he recalled years later, "Making drawings was something I liked to do, and probably it attracted attention. People said, 'Oh, he does that!'" From a very early age, Johns knew he was going to be an artist someday.

EDUCATION

Johns attended several grade schools before he spent six years in the one-room school where his aunt was the only teacher. In high school he returned to live with his mother and stepfather in Sumter, South Carolina, where he eventually graduated from high school. When Johns was 19, he went off to study at the University of South Carolina, but he was too impatient for schooling. After less than two years there, he took a bus to New York City, where he studied commercial art until he had no money left. A short time later, he was drafted into the United States Army for two years' service (1950-1952) at the time of the Korean War. He spent six months of his army service in Japan.

FIRST JOBS

After he was discharged from the army, Johns returned to New York City and got a job as a clerk in a bookshop in midtown Manhattan, where many well-known people shopped. It was only a few blocks from the great museums he dreamed of, but selling books was not the route to an art career. "I was vague and rootless," Johns later recalled. "This image of wanting to be an artist . . . was very strong. But nothing I ever did seemed to bring me any nearer to the condition of being an artist. And I did not know how to do it."

CAREER HIGHLIGHTS

A FORTUNATE FRIENDSHIP

In 1954, Johns got an unexpected break—and the start of his career as an artist—when he became friendly with one of his customers, contemporary artist Robert Rauschenberg. Already well-known, Rauschenberg had held several one-man shows. Johns called him the first serious artist he ever knew. Although their personalities were opposite—Rauschenberg was outgoing, while Johns was withdrawn—they became good friends. When an artist's loft (a large studio) became available in Rauschenberg's Greenwich Village apartment building, Johns moved in.

The two artists often visited one another, trading ideas and offering suggestions and criticisms about their paintings. They helped each other earn money as well. Rauschenberg supported himself by designing display windows for Bonwit Teller, a high-fashion Fifth Avenue department store. There was enough work for two, so Rauschenberg took on Johns as a partner. Johns was able to quit his job at the bookstore.

It was good fortune for Johns. Suddenly he was making money and had the time and spirit to begin serious painting. Determined to start anew, he destroyed the artwork that he had done up to that point in time. "I hoped to instigate a new state of affairs, to change the form of my thought and the content of my work," Johns said.

CREATING A NEW STYLE OF ART

Johns was not sure what his personal art style would be. But he was certain what it would not be: "abstract expressionism," the leading art style of the time. Abstract expressionists painted with bold strokes of color in freewheeling lines on enormous canvases, never depicting people or recognizable objects. "I didn't want to do what they did," Johns said. "I decided that if my work contained what I could identify as a likeness to other work, I would remove it."

In his studio, Johns got busy. A very slow and methodical painter, Johns would paint, repaint, and repaint again, revising his work as he went along. One day in 1957, in the upstairs apartment, Rauschenberg had a famous visitor: Leo Castelli, a noted art dealer who specialized in new artists. Castelli had planned only to discuss a show for Rauschenberg, but midway in their conversation, they went downstairs to Johns's studio. Castelli took one look at his work and was astounded. He soon set up Johns's first solo exhibit in New York City in 1958.

The public, too, was astounded. At the showing, people saw simple, stark paintings of everyday objects, created in a cool and ironic style. Johns seemed to be mocking the abstract expressionists' colorful pictures of unrecognizable forms and images. In contrast to the abstract, Johns picked simple things for his art subjects. A favorite was the American flag, painted over and over in different colors. Another subject he often chose was a bull's-eye target. Clearly, Johns was challenging abstract expressionism by showing that familiar objects could be the medium for a new creative style. As Helen Dudar explained in the *Smithsonian* magazine, "In the decade of the reign of Abstract Expressionism, this unknown

Target with Four Faces, 1955;
© 1996 Jasper Johns/Licensed by VAGA, New York, NY

young man was painting recognizable objects and symbols as common-place and thus usually as unnoticed as the linoleum on a farmhouse kitchen floor. What was exhilarating and unnerving were the sumptuous surfaces. . . . This artist had learned to control a volcanic array of emotion by keeping the imagery at bay." It was the beginning of the "pop art" movement that was to blossom in the 1960s.

Johns's first show created an immediate sensation. Some loved it, some hated it, but all were impressed. Here, Robert Rosenblum explains his initial reaction. Now an eminent art historian, Rosenblum was, at the time, a young graduate student. To this day, he remembers his first view of the Johns show. "I walked into the gallery and saw targets and flags, and my jaw dropped. I didn't know what it was. It would not compute. It had a kind of clarity about it: it was so straightforward and at the same time so unstraightforward. Everything about it was 'wrong' and didn't fit any category, and you couldn't get it out of your head."

Almost overnight, Johns became a major contemporary artist. Like Rosenblum, most critics could not believe their eyes. One critic said that in one stroke, Johns ended all the speculation about the meaning of paintings. But not all critics were so impressed. Some called Johns's work a return to "dadaism," the art movement of the early decades of the 20th century that attacked traditional artistic expression and stressed, instead, absurdity and nihilism, the belief that all existence is meaningless. But the leading people and institutions of the art world had no doubt that Johns was creating something new and important. New York's influential Museum of Modern Art, which usually waits until artists are well-known before buying their works, promptly bought three Jasper Johns paintings.

RECOGNIZABLE, YET PUZZLING, ART

As Johns once explained, his works are of "things the mind already knows." He was convinced that abstract painting had become too abstract to have any meaning. It was time, he wrote, for art to become recognizable again. Johns's idea inspired the pop artists who followed him, such as Andy Warhol. In Johns's works from the mid-1950s, the contents were recognizable, but nonetheless somewhat puzzling. In his many flag paintings, for instance, the subject is clearly the American flag, but why are they piled on top of each other, as in *Three Flags* (1958), or painted over newspaper clippings? And what is the significance of the parts of human faces that Johns painted above a bull's-eye target in *Target with Four Faces* (1955)? One of the enjoyable characteristics of a Johns painting is that viewers are likely to stop, give it a second look, and take time to interpret it for themselves.

JOHNS'S LIGHTER SIDE

Johns's seriousness as an artist has been balanced by his creative sense of humor. In 1958, he started making sculptures that were silly or sarcastic. His sculpture *The Critic Sees* (1959) shows a pair of eyeglasses that frame not two eyes but two mouths. And for the sculpture *The Critic Smiles* (1959), Johns created a toothbrush whose bristles were really teeth.

An even more whimsical sculpture was inspired by a remark of modern artist Willem de Kooning. Referring to what he felt was art dealer Leo

Castelli's lack of true artistic appreciation, de Kooning told Johns, "You could give (Castelli) two beer cans and he could sell them." Johns responded by making a bronze of two beer cans standing side by side like two ancient Greek columns. Castelli sold it for $1,000!

A NEW LOOK

Johns's reputation soared in the 1960s. His popularity during that era is explained, in part, by the fact that he was a man of his times: a rebel in rebellious times. The social structure in the United States was being transformed. America witnessed protests against the Vietnam War, rebellion against racial discrimination, and the popularity of drugs and rock music. This social revolution that would influence America for decades had its counterpart in an art revolution, and Jasper Johns was among those in its front lines. He began to do things in art that had not been done before, such as attaching actual everyday objects to his paintings. Pencils, rulers, brooms, cups, and spoons all found their way onto his work.

From the late 1960s through the 1980s, Johns's art took on an even newer look. Tired of assembling puzzling interpretations of familiar objects, Johns turned to bold new approaches. His *Untitled* (1972) used both oil paint and collage in various colors and was unified by a cross-hatching design. With its array of body parts and wooden stakes, *Untitled* has been called terrifying. During this period, cross hatchings dominated many of Johns's works.

But it was his style and subject matter, as well as his technique, that Johns was trying to change. "In my early work I tried to hide my personality, my psychological state, my emotions," Johns recalled. "This was partly due to my feelings about myself and partly due to my feelings about painting at the time. I sort of stuck to my guns for a while but eventually it seemed like a losing battle. Finally, one must simply drop the reserve."

What finally emerged was Jasper Johns the artist, struggling to innovate from recollections of his life and the lives of other artists. But critics have said that his later works remain a puzzle. With their recurring symbols based on the artist's life, Johns's later works seem "based on a code that demands to be broken, but to which he alone holds the key," commented critic Michael Kimmelman in the *New York Times*.

To "break the code," Johns offers generous clues. For example, in several paintings he portrayed women with a double image: a beautiful young woman looking backward, a sad old woman looking forward. Critics have speculated that Johns was commenting on the inevitability of growing old. "My experience of life," Johns said, "is that it's very fragmented. In one place, certain kinds of things occur, and in another place, a different kind of thing occurs."

In his mid-50s, Johns summed up his life with an autobiographical four-painting series titled *The Seasons*, first exhibited in 1987. The paintings cover the four seasons of the year, progressing from spring (youth) to winter (old age and death). The dominant image in each painting is a tracing of Johns's shadow, which was inspired by Pablo Picasso's painting, *The Shadow* (1953). The shadow is inside an artist's studio and is surrounded by things that are reminders of Johns's past. Many critics felt that Johns, as he grew older, was expressing the inevitability of death in this series of paintings.

WORLDWIDE APPRECIATION

As Johns grew as an artist, so did his public reputation. Museums began showcasing his works. Art journals assigned their senior critics to analyze his shows. In 1977, the Whitney Museum in New York City presented a huge retrospective exhibition that was later seen in San Francisco, California; Paris, France; Cologne, Germany; and Tokyo, Japan. In 1988, an extraordinary exhibition of Johns's work was included in the United States Pavilion at the Venice Art Festival in Italy.

At the same time, Johns's creations were selling for large amounts. Wealthy individuals, corporations, and museums paid large sums to own his works. In 1980, Johns's painting *Three Flags*, for which he was originally paid $600, was sold to the Whitney Museum in New York City for $1 million. At the time, it was believed to be the highest price ever paid for a work by a living artist. Johns commented that the million-dollar price "has nothing to do with painting." Yet, Johns set another record in 1988, when his 1962 painting *Diver* was auctioned for $4.2 million.

HOME AND FAMILY

Jasper Johns has always been an enthusiastic reader of philosophy, poetry, and prose. He loves to cook and play such board games as Monopoly, Scrabble, and backgammon. Because he is a very private person, some claim he is hard to get along with. His oldest friend, Robert Rauschenberg, says, "I'm not certain that he has any close friends. He's cautious and terrified of extending himself." At the same time, he is an excellent cook who enjoys entertaining. Johns lives in a townhouse in New York City and keeps a winter retreat on the Caribbean island of St. Martin. He is unmarried.

HONORS AND AWARDS

International Exhibition of Graphic Art (Ljubljana, Yugoslavia): 1965, 1966
Sao Paolo Biennale (Brazil): 1967
Skowhegan Award for Painting: 1972

Skowhegan Award for Graphics: 1978
New York City Mayor's Award of Honor for Arts and Culture: 1978
Gold Medal (American Academy and Institue of Arts and Letters): 1986
Wolf Foundation Prize (Israel): 1986
Creative Arts Award (Brandeis University): 1988
Venice Biennale: 1988, Grand Prize
National Medal of Arts (National Endowment for the Arts): 1990

FURTHER READING

BOOKS

Contemporary Artists, 1996
Crichton, Michael. *Jasper Johns,* 1977
Encyclopedia Americana, 1995
Encyclopedia Britannica, 1995
Francis, Richard. *Jasper Johns,* 1984
Steinberg, Leo. *Other Criteria,* 1972
Who's Who in America, 1996
Who's Who in American Art, 1995-96
World Book Encyclopedia, 1996

PERIODICALS

ARTNews, Sep. 1988, p.104
Current Biography Yearbook 1987
Interview, July 1990, p.96
New York Times, Oct. 30, 1988, Section 2, p.35; Mar. 1, 1991, p.C20
New York Times Magazine, June 19, 1988, p.20
New Yorker, Aug. 4, 1986, p.72; Feb. 1, 1993, p.85
Smithsonian, June 1990, p.56
Vanity Fair, Feb. 1984, p.47
Vogue, Jan. 1987, p.176

ADDRESS

Leo Castelli Gallery
420 Broadway
New York, NY 10012

Jacob Lawrence 1917-
American Artist
Painter of Scenes from African-American History

BIRTH

Jacob Armstead Lawrence was born on September 7, 1917, in Atlantic City, New Jersey. His father, Jacob Lawrence, had moved from South Carolina to the North, where job opportunities were better for African-Americans; he held a variety of jobs, including that of a coal miner and a cook on the railroad. His mother, Rosalee Armstead Lawrence, who had originally moved from Virginia, worked as a domestic servant. Jacob, the oldest of three children, had a sister, Geraldine, and a brother, William.

YOUTH

On the move trying to find steady work, the Lawrences relocated to the coal-mining town of Easton, Pennsylvania, when Jacob was two years old. But his father lost his job in the coal mines, and a temporary job as a railroad cook left him little time to spend with the family. Lack of work, constant money problems, and the difficulty of feeding and clothing three small children in these circumstances led to increasing difficulties between Jacob's parents. They separated in 1924, when Jacob was about seven, and Rosalee moved to Philadelphia, taking the children with her. Jacob remembers taking care of his little sister and brother at home while his mother was out doing housecleaning and other odd jobs. When he was ten years old, his mother left the children in foster homes in Philadelphia and moved to the Harlem section of New York City, where she hoped to find a better job. She visited the children as often as she could, but three years passed before the young Lawrences were able to move to New York to live with their mother. During the years in foster homes, Jacob vividly remembers hearing adults, like his own parents, telling stories of their experiences migrating north from different places in the Deep South.

Conscientious and independent, Jacob held up pretty well through his childhood years of poverty, a broken home, and foster care. But for a 13-year-old suddenly uprooted from familiar surroundings in Philadelphia and finding himself in the crowded Harlem ghetto, the adjustment was not easy. Schools and the neighborhood streets were dangerous and tough, and Jacob became moody and depressed. His mother, afraid that he might join a street gang, convinced her son to attend arts-and-crafts workshops after school at the 135th Street Library, and later at the near-by Utopia Neighborhood Center. The teacher at both places was African-American painter and sculptor Charles Alston, whose approach was to encourage students to have fun working with whatever materials were available. Jacob started out by painting simple squares and triangles in different colors and patterns, and then became interested for a while in making and painting papier-mâché masks. Before long, he began to cut up cardboard shipping boxes into panels on which he would paint street scenes of neighborhood tenement houses, storefronts, and billboards. Recognizing Jacob's budding talent and independence, Alston wisely left him alone to do whatever he liked and praised his efforts.

EDUCATION

After attending Pennsylvania schools in Easton and in Philadelphia during early childhood, Lawrence finished his elementary-school education in New York City at Public School 89 in 1930. He then entered Public Junior High School 139 (also known as Frederick Douglass Junior High

School) and went on to the New York High School of Commerce, but dropped out after two years. In art, Lawrence studied on and off from 1934 to 1937 at the Harlem Art Workshop, and then at the American Artists School, New York City, from 1937 to 1939.

CHOOSING A CAREER

By the time Jacob Lawrence entered high school, he had decided to major in commercial art. Meanwhile, times were hard. At the height of the economic problems of the Great Depression of the 1930s, his mother lost her job, and the family was forced to go on welfare. To make things worse, Lawrence disliked his courses in high school, most of which had little to do with art. He was 16 when he dropped out. At a low point in his life, Lawrence wound up wandering the streets looking for things he could sell. Although he did keep painting a little, he thought of art only as a hobby, not as a career. Meanwhile, he made deliveries, ran errands, and worked on a newspaper route to make ends meet and help support the family. He thought about eventually getting a job with the post office. In 1936-37, he managed to find work in construction with the Civilian Conservation Corps, a federal program that provided training and created public service jobs during the Depression.

As the family's finances improved in the mid-1930s, Lawrence began to study with Charles Alston once again, this time at the adult Harlem Art Workshop, and also took painting classes at the Harlem Community Center. He became interested in reading books and going to lectures on African-American history at the 135th Street Library. A visit to the Metropolitan Museum of Art to see a splendid exhibition of African sculpture made a deep impression on him, after which he was a frequent visitor there, walking 60 blocks each time to save money.

Lawrence soon rented some space in Alston's studio for $8 a month. There he met many well-known African-American artists, including Romare Bearden and Aaron Douglas, and writers, including Langston Hughes, Richard Wright, and Ralph Ellison. Their exchanges of ideas about art, politics, and African-American history and culture, and the contact Lawrence had with so many vital and talented people, greatly influenced him. Although still in constant need of money, working at whatever small jobs he could find, he now spent every spare moment at his easel painting. In 1937, a number of his scenes of Harlem life, including *Street Orator* (1936) and *Clinic* (1937), were shown for the first time in a group exhibit at the Harlem Artists Guild.

In 1938, through the help of African-American sculptor Augusta Savage, Lawrence was officially recognized as an artist by getting on the payroll of the Works Progress Administration (WPA) Federal Arts Project at $26 a week. At age 21, he could now paint full-time. "If Augusta Savage hadn't insisted on getting me onto the project," Lawrence later said, "I don't think I could ever have become an artist. I'd be doing a menial job somewhere." His first one-man exhibition took place that same year at the 135th Street YMCA. Lawrence's original, truthful scenes of Harlem, done in bold, direct colors and strong design with ordinary tempera paints, depicted everyday people in all the joy and suffering of urban life. These scenes won him immediate respect as a rising young talent.

CAREER HIGHLIGHTS

MAKING HISTORY INTO ART

While Lawrence was painting the people and places of Harlem, his love of books and his interest in history were taking his art into a new, quite different direction. He became deeply impressed reading about the heroic Haitian military leader Toussaint L'Ouverture, who in the late 1700s and early 1800s drove foreign rulers out of Haiti, set up a black government, and abolished slavery there. Realizing that a single portrait or scene could never fully capture either the man or those events, Lawrence completed in 1939 the *Toussaint L'Ouverture* series of 41 paintings. These paintings, along with brief captions he had written for each of them, told the complete story. Exhibited that year in Harlem, and then in Maryland at the Baltimore Museum of Art, the series won great praise.

By this time, Lawrence was already involved in the *Frederick Douglass* series, 32 paintings of the 19th-century African-American ex-slave and writer Frederick Douglass. He followed that in 1940 with the *Harriet Tubman* series, 31 paintings illustrating the career of Harriet Tubman. After her escape from slavery, Tubman helped hundreds of African-Americans escape slavery through the Underground Railroad. As in the *Toussaint* series, the paintings were all exhibited with captions written by Lawrence.

Not only powerful as art, these narrative series also brought to light for the general public important events from African-American history that had long been left out of standard elementary-school and high-school textbooks. On the strength of these works, Lawrence was awarded in 1940 the first of three Julius Rosenwald Fund fellowships. He immediately moved into a studio of his own and began to lay out what is now considered his most important series of historical narrative paintings.

THE MIGRATION OF THE NEGRO SERIES

During the years 1910 to 1930, a mass migration was taking place within the United States. Millions of African-Americans fled the rural agricultural South, hoping to escape the bigotry, poverty, racial persecution,

Strength, 1952

and even lynchings, or hangings by angry white mobs. They streamed into the urban industrial North, hoping to find new employment and a better life. Lawrence's mother and father had been part of this migration, as were his foster parents in Philadelphia. Based on library research, accounts he had heard as a child, and his own personal experiences, Lawrence told the story of this historic migration in 60 painted wood panels explained in brief, to-the-point captions. In an honest folklike style of modern art that everyone could understand, the hopes, struggles, triumphs, and disappointments of an entire people were made plain to see.

The *Migration* series was exhibited at Edith Halpert's leading Downtown Gallery in New York City in December 1941, just as the United States was entering World War II. It drew such large crowds and enthusiastic reviews that *Fortune* magazine reproduced half of the paintings in a feature article, giving Lawrence widespread coverage and winning him national acclaim at the age of 24. He was the first African-American painter to gain such recognition. (Every bit as moving and powerful as it was when first seen in 1941, the *Migration* series continued to win favorable attention in its 1993-95 exhibition held at major art museums all across the United States.) Lawrence also completed in 1942 his *John Brown* series, 22 paintings on the white abolitionist who was hanged for treason in 1859 after leading an armed assault against federal troops to advance his anti-slavery mission. In 1943, Lawrence exhibited a new group of 30 paintings depicting Harlem daily life.

MILITARY SERVICE AND THE POSTWAR PERIOD

From October 1943 to December 1945, Lawrence did wartime service in the U.S. Coast Guard and on a U.S. Navy troop transport ship in Italy, Egypt, and India. In recognition of his talent and reputation, he was given every possible opportunity to continue painting. Official Coast Guard records list 48 paintings about Coast Guard life done by Lawrence, but their present whereabouts are not known.

After leaving the service, Lawrence won a John Simon Guggenheim award and produced a *War* series of 14 paintings in 1946. He did a group of 10 works about the Deep South for *Fortune* magazine in 1947 and illustrated *One Way Ticket,* a book of poems by Langston Hughes about the African-American migration to the North, the following year. Late in 1949, due to overwork and the pressures of fame, Lawrence had a nervous breakdown and voluntarily admitted himself to Hillside Hospital in Queens, New York. During a nine-month stay there, he produced *Sanitarium,* a series of 11 paintings about his fellow patients, most of whom were white. After Lawrence's release from the hospital in 1950, the series was exhibited at the Downtown Gallery in New York. They were acclaimed as moving, sympathetic images of emotional distress. These were later followed by colorful, lighthearted works about vaudeville entertainment based on his memories of the famous Apollo Theater in Harlem.

CIVIL RIGHTS AND LIBERTIES

Throughout his career, Lawrence had been involved in the ongoing struggle for equal rights for African-Americans. His historical works and his scenes of Harlem life painted in the late 1930s and early 1940s played an important part in this struggle. Then came *Brown v. Board of Education*, the 1954 U.S. Supreme Court decision that outlawed "separate but equal" facilities for blacks and whites and barred racial segregation in public schools. This landmark victory for African-Americans inspired Lawrence to create a dramatic series of 30 paintings in 1955-56 entitled *Struggle: From the History of the American People*. Focusing on ordinary citizens rather than famous figures and depicting the struggles of blacks as part of all humanity's fight for dignity, the series pictured the attempts in America's past to establish and preserve democratic rights and freedoms. At a time of heated national debate and conflict, the *Struggle* paintings were a powerful reminder to all of basic American principles. As civil-rights issues exploded in the 1960s, Lawrence responded to violence against civil-rights advocates with angry, forceful condemnations of racial injustice. *The Ordeal of Alice* (1963), showing an African-American school-girl holding on to her books while being tormented by whites, is one example of his paintings during this time. In 1967, Lawrence also wrote the text and painted the illustrations for *Harriet and the Promised Land*, a children's book on the life of Harriet Tubman. In June 1970, the National Association for the Advancement of Colored People (NAACP) presented Lawrence with the Spingarn Medal, its highest award, for his use of art to portray the vitality of African-American life for the whole world to see.

OTHER CAREER ACHIEVEMENTS

While working as a painter, Lawrence taught art at the Pratt Institute in Brooklyn, New York, from 1955 to 1970. During those years, he also gave courses at the Art Students League and the New School for Social Research in New York City and was a visiting teacher at Brandeis University in Waltham, Massachusetts, and at California State University in Hayward. In 1971, Lawrence accepted an appointment as a full professor at the University of Washington in Seattle. He retired from teaching in 1983.

Among Lawrence's many later works are a series on African-American explorer George Washington Bush for the Washington State Capitol Museum in 1973 and a U.S. Bicentennial Celebration print in 1976. He also produced an Inauguration Ceremony print for President Jimmy Carter in 1977, illustrated a limited edition of John Hersey's book *Hiroshima* in 1983, and painted a tribute to Chicago mayor Harold Washington in 1992.

Lawrence has long been regarded as one of the finest and most original artists in the history of American art. A master in the use of color and design, he is admired for his individual style of painting as well as for his powerful themes and social message. In 1983, he was elected to the American Academy of Arts and Letters, one of the highest honors in the nation. Throughout his career, exhibitions of his works have been held

frequently all across the country, and he has received numerous other awards and honorary degrees. In 1950, when Lawrence was speaking at the Whitney Museum of American Art in New York City about the nature of art and the artist, he said, "It is more important that an artist study life than study the technique of painting exclusively. Technique will come with the desire to make oneself understood. It is more important for the artist to develop a philosophy and clarity of thought. . . . My pictures express my life and experience. I paint the things I know about, the things I have experienced. The things I have experienced extend into my national, racial, and class group. So I paint the American scene."

MARRIAGE AND FAMILY

On July 24, 1941, Lawrence married Gwendolyn Clarine Knight, whom he had met a few years earlier at the Harlem Community Art Center. She has since been his constant companion and a great help in his career from the start. "One of the most supportive people was Gwen here, who always had a feeling toward what I was doing," Lawrence has said. Gwendolyn Knight is a talented artist in her own right. In 1993, her works were exhibited in the show *Significant Others: Artist Wives of Artists* at the Kraushar Galleries in New York City. That same year, she received the National Honor Award from the Women's Caucus for Art, and in 1994, her works were seen in a solo exhibition at the Francine Seders Gallery in Seattle. The couple, who have no children, have lived in Seattle since 1971 and have traveled widely together. Although they still visit occasionally with friends in busy, bustling New York City, they now prefer the quieter lifestyle of the Pacific Northwest.

SELECTED WORKS

WRITINGS

Harriet in the Promised Land, 1968 (juvenile; also illustrator)
The Great Migration: An American Story, 1993 (juvenile)

ILLUSTRATIONS

Hughes, Langston. *One Way Ticket,* 1948
Aesop's Fables, 1970
Hersey, John. *Hiroshima,* 1983

HONORS AND AWARDS

American Negro Exposition Prize: 1940
Julius Rosenwald Fund Fellowships: 1940-42
John Simon Guggenheim Memorial Fellowship: 1946
American Academy and Institute of Arts and Letters: 1953
Chapelbrook Foundation Fellowship: 1954
Ford Foundation Grant: 1960-61
Spingarn Medal (NAACP): 1970
National Academy of Design: 1971
Books for Children Citation (Brooklyn Museum and Public Library): 1973
Commissioner (National Council of the Arts): 1978
American Academy and Institute of Arts and Letters: 1983
National Medal of Arts (National Endowment for the Arts: 1990

FURTHER READING

BOOKS

Brown, Milton W. *Jacob Lawrence,* 1974
Encyclopedia Americana, 1995
Encyclopedia Britannica, 1995
Lewis, Samella. *Jacob Lawrence,* 1982
Powell, Richard J. *Jacob Lawrence,* 1992
Wheat, Ellen Harkins. *Jacob Lawrence: American Painter,* 1986
Who's Who in America, 1996
Who's Who in American Art, 1995-96
World Book Encyclopedia, 1996

PERIODICALS

ARTNews, Jan. 1994, p.169
Booklist, Feb. 15, 1994, p.1048
Current Biography Yearbook 1988
Ebony, Sep. 1992, p.62
Modern Maturity, Aug./Sep. 1986, p.29
New York, Oct. 19, 1987, p.20
New York Times, July 28, 1986, p.A6; Oct. 11, 1986, p.B39
Time, Nov. 22, 1993, p.70
Washington Post, Apr. 4, 1987, p.C1

ADDRESS

Terry Dintenfass Gallery
50 West 57th Street
New York, NY 10019

OBITUARY

Henry Moore   1898-1986
English Sculptor
Renowned for His Monumental Sculptures
That Celebrate the Human Form

BIRTH

Henry Spencer Moore, often considered the greatest sculptor of the 20th century, was born on July 30, 1898, in Castleford, a small mining town in the Yorkshire region of England. He was the seventh of eight children of Raymond Spencer Moore and Mary Baker Moore. When his younger sister died, Henry became the youngest in the family. Henry's father was a coal

DA Vinci
School of Art!

African
influenced
artist

miner who had worked his way up to mining engineer. Henry's mother, a homemaker, was a very caring woman who did everything she could for her large family.

YOUTH

Moore's parents had a great influence on his artistic future. His father was a role model, in a way. Raymond Moore spent his early life deep in the dark underground mines, chipping away rock. Later, Henry Moore did the same thing—chipping away stone, only above ground, in the sunlight, creating works of art.

His mother's love for her children inspired much of Moore's sculpture, which focused on women, children, and family. By chance, Henry's mother provided him an early lesson in form and texture. Because Mary Moore suffered from rheumatism, an ailment that causes aches and pains, Henry often rubbed her back. "I discovered so many different hardnesses and softnesses," he later said, "so many little mountains and valleys which I got to know the way a sculptor needs to get to know things—through touch."

Another important early influence for Moore was the rugged Yorkshire countryside. Everywhere he walked, he saw jagged rocks, smooth boulders, and towering heaps of stones from the mines. To this young man's eye, these were nature's works of art. It may explain why Henry Moore's sculpture is nearly always shown outdoors and rarely exhibited in museums. He saw his art as an extension of nature and made nature a backdrop to the art.

CHOOSING A CAREER

Most people do not choose their life's work when they are still children, but Moore made his choice at the age of 11. One Sunday morning while he was attending church school, his teacher spoke of Michelangelo, the 16th-century sculptor and painter. Michelangelo created some of the greatest art works of all time, including the marble sculpture of David in Florence and the paintings on the ceiling of the Sistine Chapel at the Vatican in Rome. The teacher called Michelangelo the "world's greatest sculptor." He described to his class how the Italian master created one of his masterpieces, *Head of a Faun*. Moore, who had always liked carving wood and drawing in school, listened very intently. In that Yorkshire church that Sunday morning, Henry Moore decided to become a sculptor.

EDUCATION

Moore's father wondered if art was the correct career choice, as he doubted whether anyone could actually make a living as a sculptor. He convinced a disappointed but trusting Henry that he would be better off in a profession that offered greater financial security. With his parents' encouragement and the benefit of a scholarship, Moore began training as a teacher at the nearby Castleford Grammar School in 1910. By 1916, he had become a student teacher. During his years at the school, two teachers encouraged his artistic impulse. The headmaster, or principal, whose special interest was English church architecture, introduced him to the remarkable sculptures and stone carvings on Yorkshire churches built in the Middle Ages. And his art teacher helped him win a government grant to study art.

In 1917, during World War I, Moore left school and enlisted in the British Army. He was sent to France, where he was badly sickened by poison gas at the Battle of Cambrai. After recovering, he was returned to service, at his own request, until the war's end in November 1918. In 1919, he used his veteran's benefits to enroll in the Leeds School of Art, where he became fascinated with primitive art, especially that of Africa. In 1921, on a scholarship, Moore entered London's Royal College of Art, studying African art, early European art, and pre-Columbian art (American art done before 1500). It was there that he first began to draw from life. He also visited Italy on a traveling scholarship, spending most of his time in Florence studying the Italian masters Michelangelo, Masaccio, and Giotto. He greatly admired the monumental size of the works of Michelangelo. In 1925, after graduation, Moore joined the faculty at the Royal Art College in London and then taught at the Chelsea School of Art beginning in 1932.

Although Moore studied the classical Italian masters in Florence, many believe he found equal, if not greater, influence in the primitive artists of Africa and America. Time and again he returned to the British Museum's primitive art wing. Moore also spent many hours at London's Museum of Natural History and Geology, where he studied the structures and shapes of bones, shells, and cells in order to learn from nature.

CAREER HIGHLIGHTS

RECLINING FIGURE

In 1928, Moore mounted his first exhibition at a London gallery, but it did not attract a great deal of attention. Yet one year later, when he was 31, Moore burst upon the art world with his historic *Reclining Figure*, a sculpture of a woman resting. Many believe it was inspired by his mother. Embodying a universal theme of womankind, the woman's figure is large yet delicate, odd yet familiar. In many subsequent sculptures, Moore often returned to this theme of a reclining woman.

Reclining Figure, 1929

Many art experts believe that *Reclining Figure* was partly inspired by the hypnotic Mexican sculpture of Chacmool, the reclining figure of the tribal rain god that today still rests atop a Mayan temple in Yucatan, Mexico. Over the years, Moore would expand on this basic theme by sculpting women with children and couples with children. Some statues were nude, some were clothed, but all had a common theme—the human condition. Moore's sculptures clearly evoke the human form, but many pieces are abstract, rather than strictly realistic. They typically feature small heads, large bodies, and smooth surfaces, often with holes in the center. They combine such elements of modern abstract art with primitive concepts. In these pieces, Moore combined the simplicity of the human body with the basic theme of caring and nurturing in a way that most people find thoughtful and satisfying. Moore loved the creative process, believing that creating form out of stone, bronze, marble, wood, clay, or plaster was "like God's creating something out of nothing."

Moore had strong ideas about how his works should be shown. He believed that his sculptures looked better outdoors, in a park or plaza, than in a museum. He said that the sky and trees should be the setting and that his works should be looked at from every angle, in every light, and at every time of day. But Moore's works, like that of all popular artists, were not praised by everyone. Britain's Prince Charles once described a

Moore sculpture as "looking like a monkey's gallstone." A French sculptor said Moore "became an expert in corporate art." But historical judgment calls Moore the 20th century's most important sculptor, whose work continues to honor humanity and nature.

IMAGES OF WAR

Moore's artistic images changed dramatically in the early 1940s. Life in England was very difficult during the beginning of World War II. Although he was try to working at his sculpture and art full-time, it was tough to do. His studio was damaged by bombs, and he had no way to get large pieces of stone or wood to carve. So he began working in a different form.

During the war, German warplanes bombed London with such devastation that Londoners had to go into hiding. Children were sent off to live with friends or relatives in the country, while adults took shelter every night in the subway tunnels deep below London's streets. Every night during the bombings, thousands of Londoners would pile onto benches, onto the floor, anywhere they could find comfort, wrap themselves in blankets, and try to sleep. Moore ventured down into the subway bomb shelters one evening. He was deeply moved by the sight of all the sleeping people—huddled, bundled, heroic. They immediately reminded him of his famous reclining figures, and they inspired him to do a series of sketches called *The Shelter Drawings*, which proved immensely popular. As John Russell explained in the *New York Times*, "At a time when whole populations felt as if they were being carried in the hold of a slave ship toward an unknown destination, these drawings came across with a power and an immediacy that turned Mr. Moore from an avant-garde artist with a relatively tiny audience into someone who seemed to speak for a beleaguered nation in terms to which everyone could respond."

LARGE SCULPTURES

Following the war, Moore began to create enormous monuments, which are considered his most memorable works. Working in a variety of materials, including metal, stone, and wood, Moore sculpted some of his best-known pieces. One such piece was *The Family Group* (1948-49), one of a series of tender family portraits from the late 1940s that was inspired by his wartime experiences. Another piece, a bronze casting of his *King and Queen* (1952-53) that shows two regal figures sitting on a bench, is on the grounds of an estate that overlooks the Scottish highlands. *Draped Reclining Figure* (1952-53) was commissioned for the Time-Life Building in London. During this time, Moore also sculpted *Internal and External Forms* (1953-54) in wood. In 1956, his *Glenkiln Cross* sculpture brought together symbols of Christianity and paganism. In 1957, when Moore was commissioned by UNESCO (United Nations Educational, Scientific, and

Cultural Organization) to create a sculpture for its Paris headquarters, he carved a 60-ton block of Italian marble into a reclining figure 16 feet long. In 1964, he completed an enormous bronze figure 16 feet high and 30 feet long for New York City's Lincoln Center for the Performing Arts. Ultimately, Moore created a sculpture large enough to walk through: *Square Form with Cut*, near Prato, Italy, in 1970. Carved of white marble, it stands 18 feet high and weighs 170 tons.

Art experts have said that Moore's preference for monuments explains why his human figures usually have heads too small for the bodies. This, the experts believe, emphasizes the human body as a monument. Usually, Moore's figures are heavy and maternal. Some have holes in them, which he used as another way to define space, to relate form to emptiness. "A hole," Moore once said, "connects one side of a sculpture to another, making it immediately more three-dimensional. And the three dimensions are what sculpture is all about." He carried that theme of "sculpture voids" into a series of separated works: two smallish figures related to each other just as two humans link to one another.

PROTECTING HIS ART

Moore was an admirer of the French sculptor Auguste Rodin, creator of *The Thinker*. But unlike Rodin, Moore never permitted casting (copies made by molds) of his work after his death, which has made his sculptures more rare and thus more valuable. Yet, Moore never grew rich from his work. Late in life, he donated his personal collection of major sculptures, valued at $15 million, to the Art Gallery of Ontario in Toronto, Canada.

Moore was unconcerned about financial issues. Instead, he was determined to maintain the appropriate outdoor setting for his sculptures. He once turned down a major exhibition at New York City's Guggenheim Museum because he felt his works would be out of place in the spiral-shaped building designed by Frank Lloyd Wright, the great American architect best known for his daring designs. Moore even rejected a generous fee from New York City's Trade Center, the 110-story twin towers, because he did not believe the setting had any natural beauty.

A SIMPLE LIFE

Although famous in his native England and throughout much of the world, Moore did not act like a celebrity. He was mild mannered, hated giving speeches, and enjoyed plain talk. Once, after receiving a long introduction at a formal ceremony in New York City, Moore went to the microphone and merely said, "Thank you." Nor was he inclined to attend parties. When two art galleries were giving receptions in his honor on the same night, he sent messages to each that he was at the other

The Family Group, 1948-49

event, but did not go to either. More than once, Moore was offered a knighthood by Britain's Queen Elizabeth, but he declined. He felt that "titles change one's name and one's opinion of oneself."

Moore lived well but never grew rich. He established an art foundation to preserve and market his works and accepted only a modest salary. He lived most of his adult life in a remodeled 15th-century farmhouse in the quiet community of Much Haddam, in the rolling countryside of Hertfordshire, England, and got around town by bicycle. Moore once noticed that the sheep grazing on his land liked to scratch themselves by rubbing against a tree. Moore treated his woolly neighbors to a fancier rubbing surface: a 14-foot sculpture he called *Sheep Piece*. The critics liked it, and so did the sheep.

MARRIAGE AND FAMILY

In the postwar decade of the 1920s, students came from all over the world to study at the Royal College of Art in London. One was Irina Radetsky, who came from Russia to study painting. At a school dance one night, Irina was in the arms of her fiancé when she caught the eye of Henry Moore. For Moore, it was love at first sight. He stole her away from her fiancé and married her seven months later, in July 1929. Their daughter, Mary Spencer Moore Danovsky (born in 1946), is a book illustrator who has three children. Beginning in the mid-1960s, the Moores spent their summers in a red-tiled bungalow that Moore built in Forte dei Marmi in Italy, near the Carrara marble quarries. Moore died on August 31, 1986, at the age of 88, in the English farmhouse that had been his home for 40 years.

LEGACY

Moore's sculpture is as popular with the general public as it is with most art critics. One reason is that his usually simple figures of men, women, and children are easy to understand. What is more, the figures are often clustered together to form families. People relate to these large works of stone or bronze because they see them as artistic symbols of themselves or their families. These works, many agree, show basic truths about the human condition in a simple yet dramatic fashion. Because his tribute to the human family is appealing to all cultural backgrounds, Moore's work has been appreciated throughout the world.

Much of Moore's sculpture is seen in the plazas of skyscrapers in such major cities as New York, London, Paris, Chicago, and Toronto. City architects used his sculpture to soften the look of their large, boxy buildings. Soon, large corporations were eager to acquire Moore's sculpture. They believed his family-oriented works introduced a more warm and human element into their sometimes cold and imposing towers.

Art historians see a range of early influences on Moore's work. Some art critics link his sculpture with that of the Mayans, the artistically and scientifically advanced Central American Indians of centuries ago. Other experts see a connection between Moore's sculpture and that of Stonehenge, the mysterious circle of huge standing stones on the Salisbury plain in southern England. But whatever the influence, sculptor Henry Moore put it all together in a unique manner — sculptures that are nurturing and reassuring. The feeling of comfort his mother gave to him as a boy, he returned to the world as a man.

WRITINGS

On Sculpture, 1971

HONORS AND AWARDS

Venice Biennale Prize (Italy): 1948, for sculpture
Biennale Sao Paulo (Brazil): 1953
British Companion of Honor (England): 1955
Stefan Lochner Medal (Germany): 1957
Carnegie Prize (Carnegie Museum of Art): 1958
British Order of Merit (England): 1963
Premi Antonio Feltrinelli (Italy): 1963
Erasmus Prize (Netherlands): 1968
Grosse Goldene Ehrenzeichen (Austria): 1978
Grand Cross of the Order of Merit (Federal German Republic): 1980

FURTHER READING

BOOKS

Contemporary Artists, 1996
Encyclopedia Americana, 1995
Encyclopedia Britannica, 1995
Finn, David. *Henry Moore: Sculpture and Environment,* 1976
Gardner, Jane Mylum. *Henry Moore: From Bones and Stones to Sketches and Sculpture,* 1993 (juvenile)
Hall, Donald. *Henry Moore, the Life and Work of a Great Sculptor,* 1966
Mitchinson, David. *Henry Moore Sculpture,* 1981
Moore, Henry. *On Sculpture,* 1971
Who Was Who, Vol. IX
World Book Encyclopedia, 1996

PERIODICALS

ARTNews, Feb. 1987, p.37; May 1993, p.55
Current Biography Yearbook 1978; 1986 (obituary)
Life, May 1983, p.118
Macleans, Sep. 15, 1986, p.63
New York Times, Sep. 1, 1986, p.A1
New Yorker, July 8, 1983, p.80
Newsweek, Sep. 15, 1986, p.75
Reader's Digest, Feb. 1988, p.161
Time, Sep. 15, 1986, p.102
U.S. News & World Report, Sep. 15, 1986, p.67

OBITUARY

Grandma Moses 1860-1961
American Folk Artist
Primitivist Painter

BIRTH

Grandma Moses, the popular American folk artist, was born
Anna Mary Robertson on September 7, 1860, on a small farm
in Greenwich, New York, northwest of Troy and near New
York's border with Vermont. It was a region, she once wrote,
"back in the green meadows and wild woods." Her parents
were Russell King Robertson and Margaret Shannahan
Robertson, whose Scottish and Irish ancestors came to the

United States between 1740 and 1830. Her parents raised sheep for wool and grew flax to make linen. Anna was one of ten children.

YOUTH

During the first five years of Moses's life, Abraham Lincoln was president and the American Civil War was crippling the nation. On the Robertson farm there was little to do except work, and farm work in those days was especially hard. Throughout her youth, there was no electricity, and water was pumped from a well. There were no lights or telephones; no toilets or running water; no television or radio.

Like other farm girls of those times, Moses busied herself with such responsibilities as cleaning house, cooking, and caring for her brothers and sisters. There were many fun times as well, playing with her sisters and brothers and children from the nearby farms. There was a strong feeling of community among farm families. It was customary to help neighbors when harvesting or sheepshearing was too big a job for one family. As Moses recalled in her autobiography: "Those were happy days, free from care or worry, helping mother, rocking sister's cradle, taking sewing lessons from mother, sporting with my brothers, making rafts to float over the mill pond. [I would] roam the wild roads gathering flowers and building air castles."

EARLY MEMORIES

When there was no one to play with, Moses amused herself by drawing sketches. Her father bought sheets of white paper, the kind used for newspapers, and he liked to see the children draw pictures. One brother loved to draw steam engines, while another brother preferred animals. Moses liked to draw pictures of happy events and would color them with juice from grapes or berries, particularly red colors. Bright red was her favorite color.

EDUCATION

In farm country in the mid-1800s, work came first, and schooling was secondary. There were three months of classes in the summer and three months in the winter. As Moses recalled, however, many young children did not go to school much in winter because it was so cold, and they did not have enough clothing. This was true for Moses, and she did not receive much education.

FIRST JOBS

When she was 12 years old, Moses left home to earn her own living as what was then called "a hired girl," someone who helped out a family. It was ordinary work, but Anna liked it. She felt that it gave her an education in cooking, housekeeping, and getting to know people in the outside world. Anna went to live with an elderly couple who treated her like a member of the family. She took pride in her cooking, especially her fine dinners. When the minister came she would set out the best linen and silver along with the china tea set and serve a fine meal that she had cooked herself. After her employers died, she worked for other families, mostly caring for the sick, until she met her husband-to-be.

MARRIAGE AND FAMILY

Anna married Thomas Salmon Moses, a farmer, in the fall of 1887. They headed south after their wedding, settling on a 600-acre dairy farm in Staunton, Virginia. They had ten children, five of whom died at a very young age. Moses's time was spent caring for her family, working on the farm, making imprints on butter for area restaurants, and making and selling her potato chips. Late in life, she recalled her Virginia years: "Here I commenced to make butter in pound prints and ship it to White Sulphur Springs, West Virginia. I also made potato chips, which was a novelty in those days. . . . Here our ten children were born and there I left five little graves in that beautiful Shenandoah Valley."

In 1905, when Anna was 45, she returned to New York State with her husband and children. They bought a farm in Eagle Bridge, near her childhood home, and went into the dairy business. For the next 20 years, Moses took care of her family, her home, and the farm. In 1927, when she was 67, her husband died. Her youngest son and his wife took over the farm, and she had a lot of time on her hands. To occupy herself in her late 70s, Moses turned to art.

CAREER HIGHLIGHTS

Moses's first artistic efforts at that time were embroidering on pieces of stiff wool. It had been a talent popular among many women, young and old, in the late 1800s. She pleased many neighbors and friends by making gifts of her pictures. But by age 78, her hands were growing stiff from arthritis, a disease that makes joints painfully rigid. It was hard for her to hold the needle, so she put it aside and picked up a paintbrush.

Moses sent away to the Sears Roebuck mail-order company for a box of artist's oils and some brushes. When the mailman rode up with her package, she could not wait to open it. Her first paintings were copies of picture postcards made by Currier and Ives, two 19th-century American artists who created popular prints of early American scenes.

STARTING WITH FUNDAMENTALS

As her skill with the paintbrush developed, Moses discovered she could do more than copy the work of others. She began to create her own origi-

Grandma Moses at work on a table she has painted

nal works, many of which were based on her fine memory of the past. She recalled absolutely clearly the farm of her youth, which was nearby. Her first works included scenes of picking apples, gathering maple syrup, and catching a turkey for Thanksgiving.

Moses's pictures are simple, straightforward depictions of rural life. She used everyday figures of boys and girls and men and women, dressed in bright clothing. Her paintings, from the first to the last, always showed happy times. The subjects of her paintings work hard, play hard, and live well. They are shown celebrating holidays, playing outdoors, ice skating, and performing everyday farm chores, among other activities. Moses's paintings are often enjoyed as expressions of good and simple traditional America. The artistic message is basic and direct, and it possesses a rare quality in contemporary art: charm.

GRANDMA MOSES IS "DISCOVERED"

Anna Moses was proud of her paintings and liked to display them. In 1939 she was able to showcase some in the window of the town drugstore in nearby Hoosick Falls. Grandma Moses was "discovered" when an amateur art collector from New York City, out for a Sunday drive in the country, spotted the paintings in the store window. His name was Louis Caldor, and he regarded what he saw as a great discovery. Caldor bought all four of Moses's paintings on the spot, but he wanted more. The druggist gave him directions to the Moses farm. The next day, Caldor drove out to the farm and bought Anna Moses's entire collection — 15 paintings.

Back in New York City, however, Caldor found that there was little interest in the paintings. When he overheard talk of an art show for amateurs at New York City's famous Museum of Modern Art, he persuaded those in charge to include Moses's work. Three of her paintings were exhibited at the museum, and people loved them. Suddenly, the newspapers discovered this 79-year-old talent, whom they called "Grandma Moses." As for Caldor, he became her lifelong friend.

A year later, in 1940, Moses had a one-woman show at the Galerie St. Etienne in New York City. The exhibit included 35 of her paintings, mounted in frames from old mirrors in her farmhouse attic. The show was a sensation. Sophisticated New Yorkers suddenly began talking about the 80-year-old lady from upstate whose paintings everyone loved. Art critics quickly began analyzing her work. They noted that there were no dramatic angles, no mystifying symbols, and no sense of perspective — a way of showing distances, such as height and depth, on a flat surface, such as a painter's canvas. What the viewer saw, instead, were charming scenes of America's rural past. This type of art is called primitive art, and Grandma Moses was an "authentic American primitive artist." Primitive artists, who are usually self taught, paint in a style that is marked by freshness, directness, and naiveté.

BECOMING FAMOUS

Astonished at her overnight fame, Moses quietly remained on her farm. In the fall of 1940, she received an invitation from Gimbels, a noted Manhattan department store. They wanted to exhibit her paintings at their Thanksgiving festival and invited her to New York City for the festivities. She came by train to Grand Central Station and was amazed to see how the city had changed since she last visited there 22 years before.

Moses did not arrive in New York City empty-handed. She remembered that when she had exhibited both her fruit preserves and her paintings at a farm fair a few years earlier, she had won a prize for her jams, but her pictures were ignored. So just to be on the safe side, Grandma Moses came to the city with some home-made bread and jelly!

Hundreds of people showed up at Gimbels to see this remarkable woman. "Afterwards," she recalled, "oh, it was shake hands, shake, shake, shake —and I wouldn't even know the people now." After the hectic pace of New York City, Grandma Moses was happy to return to the peace and quiet of her farm. She continued her painting at a remarkable rate: in the 20 years of her career, she turned out more than 1,200 paintings.

PRESIDENTIAL APPROVAL

Grandma Moses's fame spread far and wide. In 1949, she was invited to Washington, D.C., to receive the Women's National Press Club Award. There was an official dinner at the Presidential Room of the Statler Hotel, and when she entered the hall, the 700 invited guests gave her a standing ovation. The next day, President and Mrs. Harry Truman invited her to tea at Blair House, where the Trumans were living while the White House was being remodeled. After the train ride home, 800 people jammed the main street of Hoosick Falls to welcome her home. Soon after, her sons built her a comfortable new home across the road from her old farmhouse.

In 1950, Grandma Moses's fame crossed the Atlantic Ocean. A collection of 50 of her paintings was shown in France, Germany, Austria, Switzerland, and the Netherlands. The noted London magazine *Art News and Review* called her "one of the key symbols of our time." About that time, Moses was persuaded to write her autobiography. After *My Life's History* came out in 1952, it was also published in England and, in translation, in Germany and the Netherlands.

One of Grandma Moses's big admirers was Dwight D. Eisenhower, who was President of the United States from 1953 to 1961 and whose hobby was painting. Some of the president's Washington friends thought it would make a great surprise gift if Grandma Moses would do a painting of Eisenhower's farm in Gettysburg, Virginia. By copying photographs of the president's farm that were sent to her, she did a painting that indeed surprised and pleased Eisenhower.

HER 100TH BIRTHDAY

Grandma Moses marked her 100th birthday at home in Eagle Bridge in 1960. Mailbags full of cards and letters swamped the post office. A few reporters were allowed to interview her and they found that she was still a remarkable woman. She remained kindly and humorous, despite her fame, and everyone noted her strong spirit.

Grandma Moses finished 25 more paintings after her 100th birthday. But within a year, her health faltered. She took a bad fall at home and entered a nursing home in Hoosick Falls, where she continued to paint until she could no longer hold a paint brush. Grandma Moses died five months later, on December 13, 1961.

LEGACY

The art of Grandma Moses is cheerful and sentimental. It portrays the American countryside as a place of down-to-earth warmth and good fellowship. But it could have been the countryside in many lands, because she chose ordinary people and everyday themes for her subjects and made them special. "The simple realism, nostalgic atmosphere, and luminous color with which Grandma Moses portrayed homely farm life and rural countryside won her a wide following," wrote the *New York Times*. "She was able to capture the excitement of winter's first snow, Thanksgiving preparations, and the new, young green of oncoming spring." Her art reflected her own philosophy of honesty and good cheer.

Grandma Moses was an extraordinary person. At 78 years old, she began two more decades of creative activity. "Her magic was that she knew how magical it was to be alive," wrote art critic John Canaday in the *New York Times*, "and in her painted records of her life she managed to relay some of this magic to the rest of us." Grandma Moses spent most of her life gathering memories and in her final years passed them on to everyone else. Her gift was art that offered everyone the innocence and happiness of a simpler time.

What is more, Grandma Moses painted all her works from memory — remarkable, considering how much she had to remember. She lived through one-half of America's history—from President Abraham Lincoln and the Civil War through President John F. Kennedy and the Cold War. In fact, immediately after her death, President Kennedy offered the following tribute: "The death of Grandma Moses removes a beloved figure from American life. The directness and vividness of her paintings restored a primitive freshness to our perception of the American scene. Both her work and her life helped our nation renew its pioneer heritage and recall its roots in the countryside and on the frontier. All Americans mourn her loss."

WRITINGS

My Life's History, 1952

HONORS AND AWARDS

New York State prize for painting (New York State Exhibition at
Syracuse Museum): 1941
Metropolitan Museum of Art Award: 1947, "for distinctive merit"
Women's National Press Club Award: 1949, "for outstanding accom-
plishment in art"

FURTHER READING

BOOKS

Armstrong, William H. *Barefoot in the Grass: The Story of Grandma Moses,*
1971 (juvenile)
Binacree, Tom. *Grandma Moses*, 1989 (juvenile)
Encyclopedia Americana, 1995
Encyclopedia Britannica, 1995
Graves, Charles P. *Grandma Moses, Favorite Painter*, 1969
Kallir, Otto. *Grandma Moses*, 1973
Kallir, Otto. *Grandma Moses: American Primitive*, 1946
Kramer, Nora. *The Grandma Moses Storybook*, 1961
Moses, Grandma. *My Life's History*, 1952
O'Neal, Zibby. *Grandma Moses: Painter of Rural America*, 1986 (juvenile)
Tompkins, Nancy. *Grandma Moses*, 1989
Who Was Who, Vol. IV
World Book Encyclopedia, 1996

PERIODICALS

Current Biography Yearbook 1949; 1962 (obituary)
New York Times, Dec 14, 1961, p.1
Newsweek, Dec. 25, 1961, p.56
People, Feb. 11, 1985, p.26
San Francisco Chronicle, Apr. 10, 1991, p.B3
Saturday Evening Post, Nov. 1983, p.62
Time, Dec. 22, 1961, p.32; Feb. 11, 1985, p.26
USA Today Magazine, July 1985, p.26
Washington Post, Feb. 12, 1979, p.D1

FILMS

Grandma Moses, 1950

OBITUARY

Louise Nevelson   1899-1988
Russian-Born American Sculptor
Creator of Wooden-Box Wall Sculptures

BIRTH

Louise Nevelson was born Leah Berliawsky in Kiev, Russia, which is now part of Ukraine. Born sometime in September 1899 (the Russian calendar was slightly different than ours), Leah celebrated her birthday on September 23. Her father, Isaac Berliawsky, was from an educated and prosperous family, living near Kiev in southwestern Russia. Although the family was in the lumber business, they were forbidden to own land because they were Jews. Her mother, Minna Ziesel (Smolerank) Berliawsky, was from a poor farming family that was part of a *shtetl*, a small isolated Jewish community. Although they were poor in material wealth, they were enriched by a strong sense of community, faith, and scholarship. Leah was the second of four children. She had two sisters, Anita and Lillian, and one brother, Nathan.

YOUTH

Three years after Nevelson was born, her father emigrated to the United States, where his sisters and brothers had already settled in search of the freedom and great opportunities offered by this nation. It took him two years to save enough money to send for his wife and children, who were staying in the *shtetl* with his in-laws in Russia. During this time, Nevelson, already a very shy and withdrawn child, became absolutely distraught at her father's absence and did not speak for six months after he left. Eventually, she came to enjoy those years living in the *shtetl* with her maternal grandparents, watching her grandmother color wool with homemade dyes made from vegetables and feeling safe and secure and loved in their small home in this close-knit Jewish community.

In 1905, Nevelson and her family traveled from Russia, across Europe, to America, first by wagon, then by train, then by boat across the Atlantic Ocean. It took several months. The unpleasantness of the time spent in the cramped and filthy cargo hold of the ship (where there was little food and almost no water) haunted her forever. The only fond memory she had of this voyage was the stopover at Liverpool, England. The family went ashore there, and Nevelson went into a candy shop filled with glass jars of various colored hard candies. The lights reflected off the glass jars and created a halo of colors, and Nevelson thought it "looked like heaven."

ROCKLAND, MAINE

The Berliawsky family settled in Rockland, Maine, a seaport and resort town on the Atlantic Ocean. Isaac had grown up in the family lumber business in Russia, so he was able to start his own lumber business. In America, however, he could own land, and he became quite successful in buying land, building a house on that land with the lumber from his mill, selling the house, and using the money to buy more land and build more houses. In this way, the Berliawsky family fit well into the growing and busy commercial town that was their new home.

Nevelson, whose name by now had been Americanized to "Louise," grew up in a house on the water—not in the exclusive wealthy area of summer homes for the Boston and New York upper classes, but near the shipyards. This section provided an exciting and ever-changing play-ground for the Berliawsky children. By the time Nevelson was ready to attend public school in Rockland, she had learned English and a new baby sister had just arrived. Nevelson decided that she did not want to be given any responsibilities to take care of the baby, so at the age of six, she stopped playing with dolls. Instead, she would play with scraps of wood that she gathered at her father's lumberyard, perhaps the beginning of the fascination with wood that would later inspire her wall sculptures.

Throughout her youth in Rockland, Nevelson never fit in with the other children. Many things set her apart—her Jewish heritage, her ability to speak Russian and Yiddish, her unusual foreign clothes, her artistic talents—and Nevelson retreated into herself and into her drawing and painting.

CHOOSING A CAREER

By the time Nevelson was six years old, it was evident that she had been "born an artist." She often sat at the kitchen table and drew pictures that were admired by her family. Her grade-school teachers cultivated her talent for drawing. In second grade, her teacher praised a drawing of a sunflower by Nevelson as "original," and even though she did not know what that meant, she knew it must be a high form of praise. At the age of nine, when the local librarian asked her what she was going to be when she grew up, Nevelson replied, "I'm going to be an artist." Then, she looked over at the life-size statue of Joan of Arc. This sculpture was the reason she went to the library—just so she could touch it. "No," she added, " I want to be a sculptor. I don't want color to help me."

EDUCATION

Nevelson never liked to read, and she was an average student in school. However, she always did well in art and took drama and dancing to over-come her shyness. She attended the public schools in Rockland, Maine.

One of Nevelson's greatest influences during her high school years was her art teacher, Lena F. Cleveland. At first, Cleveland thought that the homework Nevelson turned in for her art class had been traced, but when she eventually realized that they were Nevelson's own drawings, she encouraged her to enter art competitions. Each time Nevelson won an award, her self-confidence grew. She spent most of her free time in the art room at school. Being in that room had an additional benefit—it was the only time she was ever warm. Nevelson hated the cold, and even as an adult she felt warm only in her studio.

During her high school years, Nevelson became known for dressing with a certain dramatic flair. Several people—especially Lena Cleveland—

influenced her flamboyant style of dress, which may have been as much an artistic statement as was her sculpture. By watching Cleveland, Nevelson learned to buy clothes around a particular scarf or piece of jewelry that she loved. Also imitating her mother's style and appearance, she would walk through school with her head held high. Nevelson's mother was quite beautiful and spent hours getting dressed for the Sunday family stroll through Rockland, where she would draw admiring stares from the crowds. Nevelson copied her mother's love of hats and always had the perfect hat for each outfit. Her love of creative clothing continued throughout her life. Years later, Nevelson became known in the art world as "The Hat," although as she grew older, she exchanged her hats for fancy scarves to wear on her head. She also often wore the dress of the Pemaquid Indians, who lived near Rockland and who had stores in the seaport that Nevelson had frequently explored as a young girl.

After Nevelson graduated from high school in 1918, her art teachers recommended that she study at the Pratt Institute, a prestigious art school in New York City that Cleveland had attended. But Nevelson decided to get married instead.

MARRIAGE AND FAMILY

When Louise Berliawsky was in her last year of high school, she had to work in the community as a requirement for graduation. She worked as a secretary in a local law firm and kept the job after graduation. Through this job she met Charles Nevelson, a wealthy man 15 years older than she. In 1920, Louise and Charles were married. Charles gave her what she wanted at the time: entry into the high-society world of New York City, filled with private art lessons, classes at the Art Students League, and excursions to the theater, opera, museums, and art galleries.

Louise Nevelson gave birth to her only child, a son named Myron who everyone called Mike, when she was 21 years old. Nevelson was unprepared for motherhood. She felt trapped with the responsibilities for her son and became depressed. Although she lived in a mansion outside of the city and enjoyed frequent trips with her sister, Anita, to the theater, museums, and concerts in New York City, Nevelson felt that life with Charles was unbearable. Charles demanded that she assume the role of devoted wife and mother and not spend so much time with her art. Knowing that she could never be happy in those roles, Nevelson left Charles in 1931, after 11 years of marriage. Her son, Mike, went to live with her parents in Rockland. The end of her marriage was extremely difficult for her, yet with her mother's encouragement, she was able to leave the financial security and social position associated with being the wife of Charles Nevelson.

Separated from her husband, she pursued her art more seriously when she enrolled at a school in Munich, Germany, run by artist Hans Hofmann. This was a dangerous time for Jews to live in Germany, as Adolf Hitler had come into power, and the art school soon closed. Fortunately, Hofmann came to New York City to teach at the Art Students League, and Nevelson followed him there.

CAREER HIGHLIGHTS

LIFE AS A STRUGGLING ARTIST

Louise Nevelson spent the next 30 years in New York City, studying art, painting, sculpting, and making friends with other artists. During this time, although she had many shows of her work, she was not able to sell many pieces. She lived off the sale of many of her personal possessions. Nevelson could have worked as an artist for the government-run WPA (Works Progress Administration), which funded many new artists at that time. But she did not apply for a commission, probably because she received enough money from her parents to buy her art supplies. Nevelson once said, "There's a price for what you do and there's a price for what you don't do. It's a two-way deal."

To supplement her income, she finally went to the WPA. All they had to offer was a position as a teacher at the Flatbush Boys' Club in Brooklyn, which she accepted. Being around these fun-filled children made her miss her own son, Mike, who continued to live with her parents in Rockland. Finally, in 1936, mother and son were together again when Mike moved to New York City to attend high school. But she kept herself apart from other artists. "I was often depressed and alone, but I was functioning as my own person and that kept me going."

Nevelson was determined to become more widely known. One day in 1941, she marched into one of the top galleries in New York and invited the owner, Karl Nierendorf, to visit her studio to see her work. Nierendorf was so impressed with her sculptures and paintings that within three weeks he gave Nevelson her first major one-woman show. Most of the reviews of this show were glowing, the reviewers commenting on her obvious fascination with primitive Indian (Mayan and Aztec) and African art. But one review read, "We learned the artist is a woman, in time to check our enthusiasm. Had it been [a man] we might have hailed these sculptural expressions as by surely a great figure among moderns." Nierendorf continued his friendship with Nevelson, recognizing her talent and promoting her work during the next few years.

By the early 1940s Nevelson was becoming known throughout the New York art world, where the major art movements of that time were being

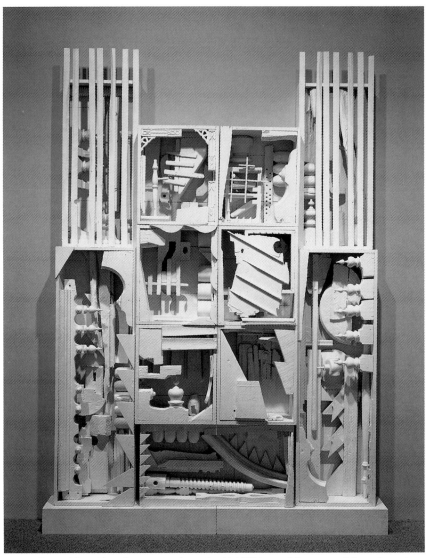

Dawn's Wedding Chapel II, 1959; photo © 1996 Whitney Museum of American Art

transplanted from war-ravaged Europe. However, this world was shattered for her in 1943 by the death of her mother, Minna. Minna had always encouraged Nevelson, had loved her unconditionally, and had supported her talent faithfully. Nevelson was so grief-stricken that she could not even attend the funeral. She sought escape from her pain by working nonstop. After days of working to exhaustion and barely eating, she would finally fall asleep. Much of her grief was let out several months later, after she had two shows with no sales. Nevelson was so angry that she burned all of her sculptures and hundreds of her paintings. She was quoted as saying, "All my life people have told me not to waste my energies on anger, but I kept anger, I tapped it and tapped it. Anger has given me great strength."

Nevelson continued to seek refuge in her work after the loss of other important people in her life. Karl Nierendorf died in 1947, and for the next two years, she worked tirelessly, developing unique and striking sculptures made from terra-cotta, a brownish-orange clay. One of her famous pieces from this period entitled *Moving-Static-Moving-Figures* was composed of geometric forms, pressed with fabric while still wet and carved with primitive faces, and then stacked on top of wooden dowels. It looked like pre-Columbian art (American art done before 1500). Her fascination with early North and Central American art was so keen that she traveled to Yucatan, Mexico, in 1950. She described Yucatan as "a world of forms that at once I felt was mine, a world where East and West met, a world of geometry and magic." When she returned from this trip, she was determined to become a famous artist and to earn a great deal of money.

THE USE OF WOOD

By the 1950s, Nevelson had experimented with many techniques and was ready for a new medium. With little money to buy her art supplies, she began scavenging the streets of New York for new materials with which to work. She rediscovered wood, a material fondly remembered from her childhood. It became a living material for her. Finding wood, in any form, with nails or holes in it, energized her. There was an additional benefit — working with wood was faster than any other medium, and Nevelson, impatient since childhood, was satisfied with the pace of these creations. She tried new things, discovering, "If I paint the pieces black, I'll be better able to see their form without any distractions." One day, she gathered dozens of empty wooden crates from the streets of New York. She arranged and assembled her other salvaged and repainted pieces of wood inside the crates, and the finished creation filled a wall. With her wall sculptures, her mark on the art world was finally established.

From the mid-1950s, she showed her work each year in one-woman shows devoted to a particular theme. In these shows, pieces of wood in all kinds of shapes were assembled into a unified whole, often within box-like structures. She created a world of shadow boxes and became known as an "architect of shadow." The effect was both startling and awe-inspiring to contemporary critics. As Hilton Kramer wrote in the *New York Times*, her wooden wall sculptures were "appalling and marvelous, utterly shocking in the way they violate our received ideas on the subject of sculpture and the confusion of genres, yet profoundly exhilarating in the way they open an entire realm of possibility." Nevelson's reputation grew when important museums purchased pieces from these early exhibits. The Whitney Museum bought *Black Majesty* from the 1956 exhibit, "The Royal Voyage," while the Museum of Modern Art took *Sky Cathedral* from the 1958 exhibit "Moon Garden + 1." Nevelson was 58 years old when she finally became famous.

SUCCESS AND FAME

From that time until her death Nevelson continued to work, experimenting with new materials in her later pieces. She also continued to display her sculptures in exhibits in the United States and around the world. She received numerous commissions and produced many large sculptures, some as tall as 55 feet, for city plazas and universities. In 1977-78, she made the all-white *Chapel of the Good Shepherd* for Saint Peter's Lutheran Church in Manhattan. In 1978, she created *Sky Gate, New York* at Manhattan's World Trade Center. In 1979, she completed the Louise Nevelson Plaza in Manhattan — a large outdoor environment composed entirely of her typical black metal sculptures. She finished a 35-foot black steel sculpture, which was installed at the National Institutes of Health in Bethesda, Maryland, just before she died on April 17, 1988, in New York City.

Throughout her career, Nevelson assumed leadership roles in many artists' associations and in 1965 participated in the National Council on Arts and Government in Washington, D.C. Yet, she remained isolated from the world in many ways. She was always devoted to her art first. "In the end," she said, "as you get older, your life is your life and you are alone with it . . . and I don't think that the outside world is needed. It doesn't have much influence on me as an artist, or on us as individuals, because one cannot be divorced from the other. It is the total life. Mine is a total life."

LEGACY

Nevelson's legacy to the art world was aptly summed up by art critic John Russell in the *New York Times*. Writing just after her death, Russell called Nevelson "a pioneer creator of environmental sculpture who became one of the world's best-known women artists. . . . She was known above all for her wall sculptures. When modern sculpture in general was getting more and more open and transparent, Mrs. Nevelson caught the public imagination by her command of darkness and deep shadow. She brought mystery back into sculpture, and the observer who stood for some time in front of one of her black walls was reminded of something not easily found in North America: the impact of carved wood and stone in a twilit Gothic cathedral. Her black walls lived in shadow and drew sustenance from it, and a large public found in her work a satisfaction that it found nowhere else in modern art."

WRITINGS

Dawns and Dusks: Taped Conversations with Diana MacKown, 1976

HONORS AND AWARDS

Tamarind Fellowship: 1963 1967
New York Citizenship Achievement Award: 1966
Carnegie Prize (Carnegie Museum of Art): 1967
Edward MacDowell Medal: 1969
Creative Arts Award (Brandeis University): 1971
Skowhegan Medal for Sculpture: 1971
Gold Medal of Honor for Visual Arts (National Arts Club): 1973
American Institute of Architects Award: 1977
Gold Medal (American Academy and Institute of Arts and Letters): 1983
National Medal of Arts (National Endowment for the Arts): 1985
Ellis Island Medal of Honor: 1986

FURTHER READING

BOOKS

Bober, Natalie S. *Breaking Tradition: The Story of Louise Nevelson,* 1984 (juvenile)
Contemporary Artists, 1996
Encyclopedia Americana, 1995
Encyclopedia Britannica, 1995
Lisle, Laurie. *Louise Nevelson: A Passionate Life,* 1990
Nevelson, Louise. D*awns and Dusks: Taped Conversations with Diana MacKown,* 1976
Who Was Who, Vol. IX
World Book Encyclopedia, 1996

PERIODICALS

Americana Annual 1989
ARTNews, Summer 1988, p.39
Current Biography Yearbook 1967; 1988 (obituary)
New York Times, Apr. 18, 1988, p.A1; Mar. 25, 1990, Section 7, p.15
New Yorker, May 9, 1988, p.27
People, May 2, 1988, p.52
Time, Jan. 12, 1981, pp.66, 71; May 2, 1988, p.69

OBITUARY

Georgia O'Keeffe 1887-1986
American Painter

BIRTH

Georgia O'Keeffe, one of America's greatest artists, was born on November 15, 1887, on her parents' farm in the wheat-growing community of Sun Prairie, Wisconsin. She was the sixth of seven children of Francis Calixtus O'Keeffe, who was Irish, and Ida (Totto) O'Keeffe, who was of Dutch and Italian descent. She had two brothers, Francis and Alexis, and four sisters, Ida, Anita, Katherine, and Claudia. Georgia was named after her maternal grandfather, Giorgio Totto, who had emigrated to the United States from Hungary, where he had lived after moving there from Italy.

YOUTH

There were several artistic influences in O'Keeffe's family. Both of her grandmothers were interested in painting. Two of her sisters were painters and one became an art teacher. Her eldest brother became an architect. Georgia was a bit shy and unconventional, but she was always determined to be herself. When she was in the eighth grade, she told a classmate, "I'm going to be an artist." By the time she graduated from high school, she was even more certain of her future, saying, "I am going to live a different life from the rest of you girls. I am going to give up everything for my art."

EDUCATION

As a young girl, O'Keeffe attended the Sacred Heart Academy convent in Madison, Wisconsin. When she was 14, her family moved to Williamsburg, Virginia, where she attended Chatham Protestant Episcopal Institute, graduating in 1904. That year, at age 17, she went off to the city to study art, first in Chicago and later in New York.

O'Keeffe started out in Chicago, where she studied with the noted instructor John Vanderpoel at the Art Institute for one year. But she withdrew after she came down with typhoid fever in the summer of 1906. The next year, her health restored, she moved to New York City to attend the Art Students League, studying with artists William Merritt Chase and Francis Luis Mora. She won a prize there for a still-life painting of a rabbit with a copper pot. But personal doubts about her work caused her to stop painting for a while. At age 22, she did some freelance commercial art in Chicago, but it did not satisfy her artistic interests.

O'Keeffe decided to become a teacher, and from 1912 to 1916, she was art supervisor in the public schools of Amarillo, Texas. She also taught art at the University of Virginia and at Columbia College in South Carolina. In the summer of 1915, she studied art at Teachers College of Columbia University in New York City, with a distinguished instructor, Arthur Dow. That summer changed her life: "It was Arthur Dow who affected my start, who helped me to find something of my own," O'Keeffe once recalled. He taught her design, how to fill space "in a beautiful way." That fall, fired up with enthusiasm, O'Keeffe returned to Texas determined to create her own individual art. She took a job as art department chair at West Texas State Normal (Teacher's) College at Canyon, Texas, and returned to her easel, painting and drawing.

BEGINNING HER CAREER

O'Keeffe did not know it, but she was about to be "discovered" by Alfred Stieglitz. One of America's most influential art figures, Stieglitz was both a noted pioneer in the field of photography and the owner of one of New York City's most famous art galleries, "291," at 291 Fifth Avenue. He is credited with establishing photography as an art form in this country and with introducing Americans to the work of such modern giants as Pablo Picasso, Paul Cezanne, Georges Braque, and Constantin Brancusi. At his gallery, Stieglitz also exhibited works by the newest and most promising of America's modern artists. One day, O'Keeffe received a letter from Anita Pollitzer, her former roommate at Teachers College in New York City, who was an admirer of Stieglitz. Pollitzer asked O'Keeffe what she had been doing lately, and O'Keeffe responded by mailing her latest charcoal sketches, with the understanding that they were private. But Pollitzer was so impressed that she showed them to Stieglitz, trying to help her friend.

"Finally, a woman on paper," responded the amazed Stieglitz, who for years had exhibited only male artists. Angered, O'Keeffe came up from Texas determined to have her drawings taken down. But Stieglitz talked her out of it. "You have no more right to withhold those pictures," he told her, "than to withdraw a child from the world." Stieglitz was intrigued by this unusual and talented artist. He took hundreds of photographs of her to exhibit in his gallery. He promoted her work and introduced her to the prominent artists of the day. As part of Stieglitz's circle, O'Keeffe was truly at the center of modern art in New York.

CAREER HIGHLIGHTS

In 1918, O'Keeffe quit teaching, moved to New York City, and began painting full-time. She joined Stieglitz's circle of artists and soon was its brightest star. She developed an artistic style so unique that she left her signature off many of her paintings. Within a few years, O'Keeffe's remarkable talent and Stieglitz's help lifted her to the heights of fame. In 1923, her first major exhibition, "One Hundred Pictures," impressed critics with its freshness and intensity. Her output was enormous—so much so that Stieglitz produced an O'Keeffe show every year until 1946, and again in 1950. The most distinguished art critic of the time, Edmund Wilson, wrote this after attending a group show: "Georgia O'Keeffe outblazes the other painters in the exhibition." In 1924, as O'Keeffe's fame was increasing, she married her friend and mentor Stieglitz.

Soon the major museums recognized O'Keeffe. The Brooklyn Museum of Art held a retrospective exhibit in 1927, and it was followed over the years by exhibits at the Art Institute of Chicago, the Museum of Modern Art in New York City, the Smithsonian Institute's National Gallery of Art, and the Dallas Museum of Fine Arts. Her paintings were bought by the Metropolitan Museum of Art, the Museum of Modern Art, the Whitney Museum in New York City, and more than 40 other American museums.

O'Keeffe and Stieglitz lived in a glamorous apartment high in the Shelton Hotel in New York City. With a grand view of the skyline, she captured in several paintings the drama of the big city. But her primary subject was nature. The couple kept a summer home at Lake George, in upstate New York, where she painted the scenery and collected the shells and rocks she would later paint in the city. O'Keeffe also loved flowers. She created hundreds of flower paintings, focusing on a single blossom that she recreated on a huge canvas in magnificent, colorful detail. Tulips, irises, calla lilies, and orchids were some of her favorites.

INFLUENCE OF NEW MEXICO

One summer, O'Keeffe traveled to New Mexico, the state nicknamed "The Land of Enchantment." She was indeed enchanted with the brilliant light, the native wildflowers, and the deserts that were the ancestral homelands of the Navajo and the Apache peoples. O'Keeffe returned summer after summer, creating what have become her most famous works: paintings of the desert with the sun-bleached bones of horned animals. The dry skull of a single longhorn steer next to a brilliant desert wildflower is a classic O'Keeffe subject.

After Stieglitz died in 1946, O'Keeffe moved to New Mexico permanently. It was there, according to art critics, that she did her most impressive work. O'Keeffe bought a rambling adobe-brick home she had admired for years. She once said it was not the solitude nor the remarkable view of the mountains that made her choose this house. It was its double door of black wood, which she painted on canvas many times. "I waited ten years to get the house, because of that door," she confessed. Outside her studio were the flower and vegetable gardens she loved to tend.

O'Keeffe remained at her New Mexico home, called "Abiquiu," for the remainder of her life. Still an active painter into the last decades of her long creative life, she also indulged her hobby of travel, visiting Europe and the Far East. When she was 74, she braved the white waters of the Colorado River on a rubber raft. She was still working at the age of 90, when she remarked about her exceptional eyesight: "I could read the tiniest type. Or see the tiniest tree on the mountain." Yet a few years later, she went blind. Nonetheless, she remained an artist, turning from painting to sculpture, modeling pottery in clay. She lived to be 98, dying in Santa Fe, New Mexico, on March 6, 1986.

MARRIAGE AND PRIVATE LIFE

When O'Keeffe married Alfred Stieglitz on December 11, 1924, she was 37 and he was 61. They were married for almost 22 years. After his death in 1946 she chose to live alone, finding companionship and inspiration in the desert. She and Stieglitz had no children; O'Keeffe always said her paintings were her children.

THE ART OF GEORGIA O'KEEFFE

Georgia O'Keeffe had many reputations: pioneer, legend, heroine, American institution. A country girl, a child of the prairies, she achieved national and international celebrity before she was 30 and continued creating critically acclaimed works of art for more than 50 years. Like other distinguished artists, she perceived in depth what others merely observed on the surface. O'Keeffe regarded her talent as genius and God-driven. She once wrote to an artist friend, "Try to paint your world as though you are the first man looking at it." Another time, she told a companion, "God told me if I painted that mountain enough, he'd give it to me."

O'Keeffe's first works were abstract—that is, they did not represent any concrete, recognizable subject. Critics have said they were early clues to her artistic imagination. She moved on to the study of flowers in blossom. Her flowers were spectacular in detail, brilliant in color, and mystically female in shape. Images from nature became her primary artistic inspiration.

O'Keeffe's greatest fame came for her paintings of barren deserts and their unique debris, bleached animal bones. To O'Keeffe, the white skulls of cattle were emblems of nature, life, and women. Her images evolved from a skull in a ditch, to a skull with a blossoming flower, and finally to a skull in the sky—an object of worship. This was to be her trademark, the horned animal's skull aloft in the clear desert sky like a family crest on a suit of armor. In these and many of her most noted works, the colors are vivid and the images are crystal clear—as if taken by a sharply focused camera. By using such a technique, she could make even the most unusual and bizarre scenes seem lifelike.

O'Keeffe had another distinction as an artist: she was American, and proud of it. Her education, technique, and inspiration were exclusively American. She chose U.S. masters for her educators. O'Keeffe was one of the very few artists in the United States who had no desire to be influenced by European artists. While the art world was adoring such European masters as Pablo Picasso and Georges Braque, O'Keeffe made a point of not visiting Europe until she was in her 60s. Embodying the pioneer style of the American West—the loner who survives against a harsh environment—her mission was to prove that the United States had its own world-class art.

O'Keeffe was also a pioneer feminist long before the equality of women was a popular view. She was an active member of the suffrage move-

Summer Days, 1936

ment, which fought to give American women the right to vote (finally achieved in 1920). For many critics, O'Keeffe's feminism was clearest in her work. Her art forms, they argue, show flowers, mountains, and valleys as they evoke the shape of the female body. Said Robert Hughes of *Time* magazine, "[One] cannot imagine the peculiar sensibility of her work—its steely finesse and suppleness, its imagery of blossoming, unfolding and embrace—coming with such conviction, or perhaps at all, from a man." Yet O'Keeffe publicly disagreed with many critics' interpretations of her work. She denied its symbolism. She also denied she was a "woman painter"—implying, of course, that her status had nothing to do with her being female. She denied that her focus on nature was related to feminism, but she once mocked male artists by doing a painting in dull, leaden colors.

LEGACY

O'Keeffe's influence on American art was profound, as Edith Evans Ashbury explained in the *New York Times* just after her death. "Georgia O'Keeffe [was] the undisputed doyenne of American painting and a leader, with her husband, Alfred Stieglitz, of a crucial phase in the development and dissemination of American modernism. . . . As an artist, Georgia O'Keeffe was a key figure in the American 20th century. . . . [She] raised the awareness of the American public to the fact that a woman could be the equal of any man in her chosen field. As an interpreter and manipulator of natural forms, as a strong and individual colorist, and as the lyric poet of her beloved New Mexico landscape, she left her mark on the history of American art and made it possible for other women to explore a new gamut of symbolism and ambiguous imagery."

But for others, O'Keeffe's influence extends beyond the art world, and into American culture as a whole. As Mark Steven wrote in *Newsweek*, "Those pioneer eyes: Georgia O'Keeffe knew what she wanted, and it was beyond the next hill. She had the gift of spiritual intensity. Like the desert air, her best work is limpid, delicate, stern. 'My first memory is of the brightness of light—light all around,' she once wrote. O'Keeffe had something else, too, granted few artists. By the time she died in Santa Fe, N.M., at the age of 98, she had become a figure of mythic consequence in American culture. Her life, art, character, and appearance—she remained beautiful—had decisively entered the American imagination. She seemed necessary."

But finally, most critics would agree that O'Keeffe's lasting legacy rests on her sensual and voluptuous paintings, as John Russell wrote in an appreciation in the *New York Times*: "[In] the end, she is likely to be remembered above all for the quite small but immensely potent evocations of landscape and natural form that still have some of their secrets intact."

WRITINGS

Georgia O'Keeffe, 1977

HONORS AND AWARDS

Induction into American Academy of Arts and Letters: 1962
Creative Arts Award (Brandeis University): 1963

Gold Medal (American Academy and Institute of Arts and Letters): 1970
Edward MacDowell Medal: 1972
Skowhegan Award: 1973
Presidential Medal of Freedom: 1977
National Medal of Arts (National Endowment for the Arts): 1985

FURTHER READING

BOOKS

Brooks, Philip. *Georgia O'Keeffe: An Adventurous Spirit,* 1995 (juvenile)
Bry, Doris, and Nicholas Callaway (editors). *Georgia O'Keeffe in the West,*
  1989
Contemporary Artists, 1996
Eisler, Benita. *O'Keeffe and Stieglitz: An American Romance,* 1991
Eldredge, Charles C. *Georgia O'Keeffe,* 1991
Encyclopedia Americana, 1995
Encyclopedia Britannica, 1995
Gherson, Beverly. *Georgia O'Keeffe: The Wideness and Wonder of Her World,*
  1986 (juvenile)
Hogrefe, Jeffrey. *Georgia O'Keeffe: The Life of an American Legend,* 1992
Nicholson, Lois. *Georgia O'Keeffe,* 1995 (juvenile)
O'Keeffe, Georgia. *Georgia O'Keeffe,* 1977
Robinson, Roxana. *Georgia O'Keeffe: A Life,* 1989
Turner, Robyn. *Georgia O'Keeffe,* 1991 (juvenile)
Venezia, Mike. *Georgia O'Keeffe,* 1993 (juvenile)
Who Was Who, Vol. IX
World Book Encyclopedia, 1996

PERIODICALS

ARTNews, Apr. 1992, p.100
Chicago Tribune, Mar. 8, 1986, p.C6; May 6, 1990, p.C1
Chicago Tribune Sunday Magazine, Feb. 28, 1988, p.16
Current Biography Yearbook 1964; 1986 (obituary)
Museum of Art Bulletin, Fall 1984 (entire issue)
New York Times, Mar. 7, 1986, p.A1
Newsweek, Mar. 17, 1986, p.77
Smithsonian, Nov. 1987, p.154
Time, Mar. 17, 1986, p.83
Vogue, May 1986, p.290; Oct. 1987, p.432
Washington Post, Mar. 7, 1986, p.D1

FILMS

Georgia O'Keeffe, 1977

Gordon Parks 1912-
American Photographer, Filmmaker,
Cinematographer, Composer, and Writer

BIRTH

Gordon Roger Alexander Buchanan Parks was born on
November 30, 1912, in the small town of Fort Scott, Kansas,
the last of 15 children of Andrew Jackson Parks and Sarah
(Ross) Parks. They were a poor African-American farm family in a time and place where racial discrimination was an
everyday condition.

At that time, their community was segregated, and blacks and
whites lived separate lives. In fact, blacks were considered in-

ferior to white people. African-Americans couldn't use most public facilities, couldn't get a decent job, couldn't get a quality education, and couldn't get any respect. In addition, African-Americans lived in fear of mob violence, and even lynchings, by whites. At that time in America, bigotry was so pervasive in some communities that whites could hurt or even kill blacks without fear of reprisal from the police or the court system.

YOUTH

Despite this climate of fear and hate, the Parkses were a strong and loving family. Andrew was a quiet father who rarely spoke to his children, but Gordon has said, "I loved him in spite of his silence." Gordon spent a lot of time with his father then. "I'd ride with him a lot [herding cattle]. . . . The kind of mustache I wear now is the kind he had." Gordon recalled that his parents filled the children with love and a strong background in the Methodist religion. "The love of this family eased the burden of being black," he said.

Sarah Parks was the anchor of the family. "My mother had freed me from the curse of inferiority . . . by not allowing me to take refuge in the excuse that I had been born black," Gordon once said. She told her son that poverty and bigotry would never go away, but they could be fought on even terms. The significant thing, she told him, "was a choice of weapons." It was good advice. For the battles to come, Gordon Parks's weapons included pride, determination, and remarkable talents.

In 1927, Parks's sense of security was shattered when his mother died. He was only 15. He spent the night lying next to her coffin, an experience he remembered as terrifying yet "strangely reassuring." He went to live with his married sister, Maggie, in St. Paul, Minnesota, but his sister's husband did not like him. A few weeks before Christmas, this brother-in-law angrily threw Parks out of the house, actually tossing his belongings out of a second-floor window. It was devastating. Without friends, without money, without much schooling, and in a region unfriendly to African-Americans, Gordon Parks had to support himself any way he could.

EDUCATION

Parks had very little formal education. He attended school in Fort Scott, Kansas, until 1927, when his mother died. As he moved about in the year that followed, he tried to complete high school, but finally had to drop out in order to earn money for food.

FIRST JOBS

Life for Parks was hard. Sometimes he slept on the streets. He took jobs as a waiter in a restaurant, a janitor in a flophouse, and a piano player in a bar. In 1929, his father and some of his sisters moved to St. Paul, so he moved in with them and went to high school. But there was never enough money. Desperate, Parks once tried robbery. He jumped on a trolley car, pulled out a knife, and pointed it at the conductor. Suddenly, all his mother's teachings and warnings came back to him. Trembling, Gordon stammered, "Conductor, would you give me a dollar for this knife? I'm hungry and don't have anyplace to stay." The conductor told him to put away the knife and offered him two dollars. Parks later wrote, "I refused the money, jumped out of the [trolley] car, and hurried away, more frightened and more ashamed than I had ever been in my life."

Parks was determined to get by; surviving seemed more important than going to school. Although he had dropped out of high school, he was still anxious to learn, and he often went to the public libraries to borrow books on a variety of subjects. He also went to art museums and studied the French impressionist masters Edouard Manet and Claude Monet. He tried his hand at painting, sculpture, and writing. He filled notebooks with melancholy songs. He was also a good enough athlete to play semi-professional basketball.

The pace Parks had set for himself was too much. In 1931, he collapsed from exhaustion and was confined to bed for six months. He had to slow down. "I couldn't escape my fate by trying to outrun it," he later explained.

After he got well, Parks took a job as a waiter in St. Paul's nicest hotel. There, at the age of 20, after years of struggle, he got his first break. The hotel bandleader overheard him at the piano playing "No Love," one of his own songs. The bandleader was so impressed that in late 1932 he offered Parks a job touring with the otherwise all-white band. Reaching New York City in 1933, the band broke up and Parks was stranded in Harlem without a dime.

At this time the nation was suffering through the Great Depression, a period of severe economic crisis in which many Americans were out of work and were desperately poor. The U.S. government had just established the Civilian Conservation Corps (CCC) to provide work for the unemployed. Parks landed a job with the CCC and married his first wife, Sally Alvis. A year later, they moved in with her parents in Minneapolis, Minnesota. Parks got a job as a waiter on the railroad, a move that would change his life.

BECOMING A PHOTOGRAPHER

One night, as the train was rolling between Minneapolis and Chicago, Parks picked up a copy of *Life* magazine that someone had left behind. In it was a fascinating picture story about poor migrant farmers, told in stark black-and-white photographs taken by Ben Shahn, Dorothea Lange, and other well-known photographers of the time. Parks could not put it down. Soon after, in 1937, during a stopover in Chicago, Parks went to a movie and saw a newsreel of war in China. It gave him the same feeling as had the photos in the magazine. "Suddenly I became aware of all the things I could say through this medium," Parks recalled. "I sat through another show, and even before I left the theater I had made up my mind to become a professional photographer."

The next week, Parks bought his first camera, a used Voightlander Brilliant, for $12.50. Within two months, he had his first exhibit—at a camera store in Minneapolis. He started taking pictures of attractive female friends, and several of those photos were published in St. Paul's African-American newspapers. His fashion photography for a department store caught the eye of Marva Louis, wife of the famous African-American heavyweight boxing champion Joe Louis. She advised Parks that he could do better in Chicago. Parks took her advice and moved. There, Mrs. Louis introduced him to several influential people. Before long, Parks was making a good living taking portraits of society women, both blacks and whites.

Parks's photographs of beautiful women paid quite well, but another side of Chicago was closer to his heart: the teeming black ghetto called the South Side. Parks recalled that "there among the squalid, rickety tenements that housed the poor, a new way of seeing and feeling opened up to me . . . it was like bruises on the face of humanity." An exhibit of his South Side ghetto photos in 1941 earned him a $200-a-month fellowship in photography from the Julius Rosenwald Foundation. Now he could do what he wanted.

CAREER HIGHLIGHTS

THE FARM SECURITY ADMINISTRATION

Parks remembered the gripping pictures of migrant families he had seen in *Life* magazine years before. He decided this type of photography was to be his specialty. In 1942, he went to Washington, D.C., and was hired at the Farm Security Administration (FSA), joining a pioneering team of photographers (including Dorothea Lange and Walker Evans) who were documenting rural poverty in America.

On his first day in Washington, Parks had a bitter experience with prejudice. Walking around the capital, he found that no restaurant would serve him, no movie theater would sell him a ticket, and no clothing store would allow him to try on apparel. Parks told his new boss, Roy

Willie Causey family at home in Shady Grove, Alabama, 1956

Stryker, "Mississippi couldn't be much worse." Stryker could only say, "Bigots have a way of looking like everyone else. You have to get at the source of their bigotry. . . . That's what you'll have to work at. [Our photographers] are out there trying to do something about those problems. That's what you must do eventually."

Stryker was persuasive, and Parks decided to stick with the FSA job. During 1942 and 1943, he traveled all over the United States documenting the good and the bad. "It was during those years that I learned the power the camera has," he recalled. His first photograph for the FSA showcased that power. Called "American Gothic, Washington, D.C.," it was a takeoff on the famous painting by Grant Wood called *American Gothic*. In Wood's painting, a rather severe looking farm couple stands holding a pitchfork. In Parks's photo, Mrs. Ella Watson, a poor black charwoman, holds a broom and mop standing in front of the American flag. "I learned how to fight the evil of poverty—along with the evil of racism—with the camera. 'American Gothic' expresses that more than any other photograph I have taken."

Because the government work for the FSA did not pay very well, Parks earned extra money in the 1940s by writing textbooks and taking photos for the fashion magazines *Vogue* and *Glamour*. During World War II, Parks also served as a correspondent for the Office of War Information.

LIFE MAGAZINE

In 1948, Parks made his move to the big time: *Life* magazine, where he began a 20-year career. In those days, before television brought news-reels into American homes, the widely read weekly magazine was the photo-news messenger to millions of subscribers. *Life* sent Parks to Paris, France, for two years. After he returned to the United States, he covered more than 300 stories, including acclaimed photo essays on the African-American civil-rights movement of the 1960s.

This work was far more relevant for him than fashion photography, but it was also more dangerous. Parks recalled receiving a death threat after taking a *Life* photo series of Malcolm X, the Black Muslim leader assassi-nated in 1965. *Life* magazine sent Parks's family out of the country and put up Parks in an elegant hotel in New York, with a 24-hour guard. "I lived like that for several months until one day I snuck out, got into my XKE Jaguar, went up to Harlem to talk to the people who were threaten-ing me and sorted things out myself."

HOLLYWOOD

Parks is a born storyteller, and his best story is his own life. He wrote his first autobiography in 1963, but he felt there was so much to tell, he wrote three more. It was the first, *The Learning Tree* (actually an autobio-graphical novel), that caught the attention of Hollywood. A friend, actor John Cassavetes, told him that the book would make a great movie and that Parks should seek out the directorship for such a project. Cassavetes set up a meeting for Parks with the executive in charge of Warner Brothers Studios. Parks thought that the meeting would be a waste of time; Hollywood had never had an African-American film director. But when Parks walked into the office, the first words out of the executive's mouth were, "How long will it take you to get out of here and start pro-duction?" Before he left the room, Parks had the green light to write the screenplay, direct the film, score the music, and be the executive produc-er. *The Learning Tree*, released in 1969, was a great success and was later chosen by the Library of Congress as one of the 25 most significant American motion pictures.

The success of *The Learning Tree* and the personal satisfaction he received from it inspired Parks to quit *Life* magazine in 1968 and concentrate on his new career as a filmmaker. His next directorial project was for Metro-Goldwyn-Mayer Studios. The movie was *Shaft*, the story of a smooth Harlem detective, played by African-American model Richard Round-tree. The smash action film of 1971, *Shaft* not only made millions, but Parks said it was inspirational: "It was a film that could give black youth their first cinematic hero comparable to James Cagney or Humphrey Bogart." There were two sequels to *Shaft*, including one directed by Gordon Parks, Jr., who gave his dad a bit part in the film.

LATER YEARS

Never content to be confined to one avenue of creativity, Parks has always followed his own paths of interest. Throughout his photographic career, he also cultivated his musical talent, teaching himself composition and writing piano sonatas, symphonies, and a ballet. At the age of 82, Parks found another outlet for his seemingly endless energy and talent: painting. In 1994, he published *Arias in Silence*, a portfolio combining photography, poetry, and painting. He collected such simple natural objects as flowers and seashells and photographed them in front of watercolor backgrounds he painted.

Why this effort at 82? "I wanted to work with beautiful and peaceful things," Parks said. "I have photographed so much crime and poverty that I needed some visual relief. Despite the brutality I've seen and faced, I am a romantic—have been all my life."

LEGACY

Gordon Parks has had a phenomenal career. In his lifetime, Parks has taken hundreds of legendary photographs; has directed popular Hollywood movies and television documentaries; has written biographies, novels, and poetry; has composed symphonies; has scored a ballet; has played semiprofessional basketball; and has sung with a band. He has won more than 50 awards and 19 honorary degrees.

Parks is what people call a self-made man. He talked his way into most of his jobs and succeeded. He taught himself to take pictures, to play and compose music, to write prose and poetry, and to make films. From the man behind snapshots of farmers' poverty, he evolved into a maker of dramatic films. From singing blues in a band, be progressed to writing a ballet in honor of civil-rights leader Martin Luther King, Jr.

The background of this legendary artist reveals much about his character, his determination, and the nature of his work. As Parks explained to a Los Angeles reporter in 1994, he grew up poor, yet family life was good and his parents never quarreled. But life was harsh. "Kansas," he re-called, "was supposedly a free state, but I couldn't take my girlfriend to the drugstore for a soda. . . . I can remember the advisers at school telling black kids, 'Don't worry about graduating—it doesn't matter, because you're gonna be porters and maids.' There were lynchings in Kansas, too. At the time, I wasn't aware I was converting those ugly experiences into fuel, but in retrospect I can see that the racism I experienced as a child gave me my drive."

The effects of racial hatred left Parks filled with a rage that, for many years, was buried deep inside of him and that tormented him with many nights of sleeplessness and bad dreams. Eventually, the torment turned to creativity. "The rage," he has said, "is mixed up with a lot of things—the writing, the music, pictures—and I have nightmares of landscapes of fire."

MARRIAGE AND FAMILY

Parks has been married three times. He married his first wife, Sally Alvis, in 1933; they were divorced in 1961. The next year, he married his second wife, Liz Campbell, whom he divorced in 1973. Later in 1973, he married Genevieve Young, whom he divorced in 1979. Parks, who has been called somewhat of a ladies' man, once explained, "The marriages ended because I'm a bad boy. Doing the kind of work I do makes it tremendously difficult to have a stable personal life."

By his first marriage, Parks had three children (Gordon, Jr.; Toni; and David); by his second marriage, he had one child (Leslie). Parks was dev-astated when his filmmaker son Gordon died in a plane crash near Nairobi, Kenya, at the age of 44.

HOBBIES AND OTHER INTERESTS

Parks grew up herding cattle on horseback, and he has continued riding for recreation as an adult. He also enjoys skiing and playing tennis.

SELECTED WORKS

AUTOBIOGRAPHIES

The Learning Tree, 1963
A Choice of Weapons, 1966
To Smile in Autumn, 1979
Voices in the Mirror, 1990

FICTION

Shannon, 1981

NONFICTION

Flash Photography, 1947
Camera Portraits: Techniques and Principles of Documentary Portraiture, 1948
Born Black, 1971
Flavio, 1978

POETRY

Gordon Parks: A Poet and His Camera, 1968
Whispers of Intimate Things, 1971
In Love, 1971
Moments Without Proper Names, 1975
Arias in Silence, 1994

HONORS AND AWARDS

Julius Rosenwald Fellowship in Photography: 1942
Frederic W. Brehm Award: 1962
School of Journalism Prize (Syracuse University): 1963
Philadelphia Museum of Art Award: 1964
Mass Media Award (National Council of Christians and Jews): 1964
Art Directors Club of New York Award: 1964, 1968
Carr Van Anda Award (Scripps School of Journalism, Ohio University): 1970
Spingarn Medal (National Association for the Advancement of Colored People): 1972
NAACP Hall of Fame: 1984
National Medal of Arts (National Endowment for the Arts): 1988
Joseph A. Sprague Memorial Award (National Press Photographers Association): 1988
Infinity Award (International Center of Photography): 1990

FURTHER READING

BOOKS

Berry, S. L. *Gordon Parks,* 1991 (juvenile)
Contemporary Photographers, 1995
Encyclopedia Americana, 1995
Parks, Gordon. *Choice of Weapons,* 1966
Parks, Gordon. *The Learning Tree,* 1963
Parks, Gordon. *To Smile in Autumn,* 1979
Parks, Gordon. *Voices in the Mirror,* 1990
Turk, Midge. *Gordon Parks,* 1971 (juvenile)
Who's Who in America, 1996

PERIODICALS

Current Biography Yearbook 1968; 1992
Detroit Free Press, Jan. 9, 1991, p.C3
Detroit News, Dec. 19, 1990, p.G3
Life, Oct. 1994, p.26
Los Angeles Times, Dec. 4, 1990, p.E2; Nov. 13, 1994, Calendar Section, p.6
Newsweek, Apr. 29, 1968, p.84
New York Times, Jan. 8, 1991, p.C15
New York Times Book Review, Dec. 9, 1990, Section 7, p.19
Smithsonian, Apr. 1989, p.66

ADDRESS

Creative Management Associates
9255 Sunset Boulevard
Los Angeles, CA 90069

I.M. Pei   1917-
Chinese-American Architect
Architect of the John F. Kennedy Library
and Other Prominent Works of Modern
Architecture

BIRTH

I.M. Pei (pronounced Pay) was born on April 26, 1917, in
Canton, China. His father, Tsuyee Pei, was a prominent
banker; his mother, Lien Kwun Chwong, died during his
childhood. I.M. stands for Ieoh Ming, which means "to inscribe [write] brightly." For most of his life, he has been
known by these initials only. His family included two sisters,
Yuen Hua and Wei, and two brothers, Kwun and Chung.

YOUTH

Pei spent most of his childhood in Canton and Hong Kong until his family moved to Shanghai in 1927, when his father became the manager of the Bank of China's main office. Pei had a traditional Chinese relationship with his father, one that was distant and in which little affection was shown, but he was very close to his mother. When he was only 13, his mother died after a long and painful illness. During the summers, the Peis visited his many relatives in the family's ancestral home city of Suzhou, northwest of Shanghai. The formal gardens of the family's luxurious summer home sparked Pei's fascination with the relationship between landscape and the placement of structures on it.

EDUCATION

In Shanghai, Pei attended Saint John's Middle School, which was like an American high school and which was run by Protestant missionaries. The students at Saint John's came from prominent families, and the course of study was demanding. Many of the students attended foreign colleges after graduation. Pei's father wanted him to go to college in England, and he passed the entrance examinations for Oxford University there. To his father's displeasure, though, he chose to enroll at the University of Pennsylvania in the United States in 1935.

Although his father wanted him to become a doctor, Pei decided to study architecture at the University of Pennsylvania. Pei was unhappy when he realized that he would be required to study drawing and painting in order to remain an architecture student. He saw that his fellow students had these talents while he did not, so, that same year, he transferred to the Massachusetts Institute of Technology (MIT) to study engineering. There, the dean of the school of architecture noticed Pei's talent for design and persuaded him to focus on architectural engineering.

During summer vacation from college in 1938, Pei made a pilgrimage, of sorts. He drove to Wisconsin, hoping to meet the famous architect, Frank Lloyd Wright. When he finally arrived at Wright's home, which is called Taliesin, Wright was away. Disappointed, Pei continued across the continent to Los Angeles, where he found work in an architect's office for the remainder of his summer break. Returning to Boston, Pei continued his architectural studies at MIT. He received his bachelor's degree in architecture from MIT in 1940.

THE WAR YEARS

By the time Pei completed his bachelor's degree World War II had started, and Japan had invaded and occupied China. Upon the advice of his father, Pei did not return to China as he had planned. Instead, he stayed in the United States and worked for a Boston engineering firm, where he learned construction techniques that would help him later with his architectural designs. In 1942, Pei resumed his studies, this time at the Harvard University Graduate School of Design, where German architect Walter Gropius was head of the architecture department. In 1943, however, Pei took a break from his studies to do volunteer work with the National Defense Research Committee in Princeton, New Jersey. Ironically, he was given the unpleasant task of designing ways for U.S. air forces to destroy bridges in Europe and to burn down buildings in Japan, the enemy of his homeland, China. Pei returned to Harvard in 1945 to continue his studies. At the same time, he also taught classes in design to the graduate students. In 1946, Pei was awarded a master's degree in architecture.

CHOOSING A CAREER

Pei's plans to return to China after finishing his master's degree were stalled again. His father advised him not to return, because China had by then become a Communist country. Pei chose not to return to a land in which he would have few freedoms. Consequently, he became a U.S. citizen in 1954. Meanwhile, Pei continued to teach at Harvard Graduate School of Design until 1948, when he began his career as an architect.

MAJOR INFLUENCES

Pei gives credit to two early teachers for their impact on his work: Walter Gropius and Marcel Breuer, with whom he had studied at Harvard. It was Gropius who, in 1919, had founded the famous Bauhaus school of design in Germany, which was closed by Germany's Nazi government in 1933. Gropius's ideal was that each design should be individualized, based on the needs of the specific project, and should incorporate modern techniques and materials for construction. While there is certainly evidence of the influence of the Bauhaus in Pei's work, his buildings also reflect his love of the interactions of light, texture, sun, and shadow, a legacy from the memories of his youth and the teachings of Breuer.

Pei studied design during the modernist tradition in architecture, which developed in the early and mid-1900s and was characterized by the need to synchronize modern living style with form. Designs were simple and geometric, and construction utilized the modern elements of glass, steel, and poured concrete. Later, during the 1960s, the reaction to the cold, impersonal modernist style created what came to be called a "postmodernist" school of design. This movement emphasized a return to the basic elements of construction: brick, stone, and wood.

Pei became a "classic modernist" in the postmodern age of architecture because the design of his buildings, while abstract, are functional and use contemporary construction materials. His style, Pei has said, is one of "enduring quality. . . . It may not look fashionable at the moment. Ten years from now it may look better. Twenty years from now, it may even look right."

CAREER HIGHLIGHTS

In 1948, Pei earned his first job as an architect, beginning a career as an internationally renowned architect that has spanned almost 50 years. In that year he was hired by William Zeckendorf of New York City, who was then the most prominent real-estate developer in the United States. Zeckendorf wanted to construct buildings in addition to buying and selling them, and he hired Pei to fulfill this dream. Zeckendorf's renovation of large sections of cities represented the beginning of modern urban renewal in the United States. Soon after, Pei became head of the architectural division of Webb & Knapp, Zeckendorf's real-estate firm. One of its first major projects was Courthouse Square, in Denver, Colorado. This group of stores, hotels, offices, and parking spaces was combined into what Pei termed a "unified building envelope expression," meaning that the buildings in the complex, no matter what their purpose, were all built in the same style to suit all tenants, then and in the future.

When Pei left Webb & Knapp in 1955 to form his own company, I.M. Pei & Partners, he continued to combine commercial and residential structures into highly acclaimed urban developments, always working within strict budget limitations. Well-known Pei projects from this time are the Mile High Center (1955) in Denver; the Place Ville-Marie (1961) in Montreal, Canada; the Kips Bay Plaza (1962) on Manhattan's East Side in New York City; and the Society Hill project (1964) in Philadelphia.

Once established in his own firm, Pei started to concentrate on single-purpose structures, for which he became most famous. The first large project for his firm was the National Center for Atmospheric Research (1967) in Boulder, Colorado. These buildings are located outside the city on an isolated hilltop. In the openness of this western landscape, with the Rocky Mountains on the horizon, Pei designed concrete buildings of reddish-brown geometric forms that remind the viewer of the Anasazi Indian pueblos of the Southwest.

By this time, Pei was well on his way to having a major impact on the architectural world. His style, which took from the best of many architects, was evolving as his own. Pei's buildings — with open spaces scattered about to encourage meetings and conversations and with inner and outer walls in simple geometric shapes — resulted from the people and activities that would occupy them and from the lay of the land that surrounded them.

John F. Kennedy Memorial Library, 1964

In 1964, Pei was chosen to design the John F. Kennedy Library at Harvard by the late president's widow, Jacqueline Kennedy (who later became Jacqueline Kennedy Onassis). Although there was no formal competition for this commission, Mrs. Kennedy had previously considered several other prominent architects, including Louis Kahn, Mies van der Rohe, and Philip Johnson. With his charm and personality, Pei was able to convince Mrs. Kennedy that he could be trusted with her vision of what the library should be. In fact, before her first visit to Pei's firm, he had his office repainted in white and decorated only with an enormous vase of flowers after he had researched her preferences in interior design.

As an architectural project, the Kennedy Library was plagued with numerous hurdles. In the planning stages, there was general disagreement on the location for the building. At one point, three different sites were selected for the library. Because Pei wanted to create a unity between the land and the building, integrating the building design into the specific landscape, he had to design a different building for each site. Finally, in 1979, the building, with its assorted geometric wings, was completed on its chosen site on the shore of the Charles River in Cambridge, Massachusetts. It received both good and bad reviews.

During the late 1960s and early 1970s, Pei designed many museums, the most famous of which is the East Building annex of the National Gallery of Art in Washington, D.C. It opened in 1978, ten years after the commission, and cost $94 million, most of which was contributed by the Mellon family. The annex was designed to consist of two triangles covered in the same pink marble as the original building. Pei's standards of perfection and his attention to detail were reflected in his demand that this marble be extracted from the same quarry in Tennessee that had provided the original marble. However, much architectural debate was generated by the sharp contrast in design between the East Building's sharp angles and the bulk and symmetry of the original building.

Meanwhile, Pei's firm remained in the public eye by obtaining commissions for notable landmarks. The massive glass and steel domestic terminal at John F. Kennedy International Airport in New York City was completed in 1970. Three years later, his firm designed the John Hancock Building in Boston. The architectural intent was to mirror historic Copley Square in the blue-green glass windows of the towering 60-story building. Unfortunately, the glass panes would not stay in place and tumbled dangerously to the sidewalks and streets below. The Hancock Building glass disaster led to expensive legal costs. Pei had to share in the responsibility, although it was later determined that the fault lay in mistakes made in the manufacturing of the glass. This costly event could have resulted in the financial collapse of Pei's firm had it not been for many foreign commissions that, in his own words, "kept [the firm] alive."

In 1976, Pei was chosen by French president Francois Mitterrand to create a new entrance to the Louvre Museum in Paris. The Louvre, one of the most famed and historic museums in Europe, is a large, squared-off, horseshoe-shaped building with an open courtyard in the center. The new entrance was to be practical as well as attractive. After studying the history of French architecture, Pei selected a pyramid shape, in which the form of the triangle was often repeated. He decided to place the pyramid entrance in the center courtyard. At first, the notion of a modern 71-foot glass pyramid placed in the center courtyard of this historic building caused an outrage. In addition, many French people were offended that President Mitterrand had given this important work to a foreign architect. Despite the criticism, Pei continued to defend his design, noting that the pyramid form was inherently strong and stable. By the time of the public opening in 1989, much of the criticism had changed to applause for the abstract elegance of the work. And now the $330 million glass pyramid, like the Eiffel Tower, has become a famous symbol of Paris.

Another controversial building by Pei opened in 1989 in Dallas, Texas. The Morton H. Meyerson Symphony Center, known as "the Mort," represented Pei's first attempt at designing a symphony hall. Before the design was accepted, Pei had to overcome many concerns about the acoustics of the center's concert hall. Finally, the shoebox-shaped hall, to be built with Indiana limestone and Italian marble, was angled on its side and surrounded with curves of glass. Then, because of escalating costs, Pei had to make compromises in the construction materials, such as brick instead of limestone and carpet instead of Italian marble. However, at the last minute, businessman Ross Perot's contribution of $10 million, along with other funds, allowed the use of the soft Indiana limestone and the Italian marble that Pei had originally selected. The concert hall itself is softened by paneled walls of African makore wood and American cherry. The finished interior lobby is awash with sunlight during the day and glows from the inside after dark.

The end of the 1980s also saw the completion of many other Pei projects, including the Creative Artists Agency in Hollywood, the science building at the Choate-Rosemary Hall School in Wallingford, Connecticut, and the Jacob K. Javits Convention Center in New York City. The Javits Center was to provide the largest exhibition space yet built in the United States and had to be constructed under a tight budget and deadline. The result (two years behind schedule) consisted of a huge central exhibition hall — big enough to contain the Statute of Liberty or two 747 jumbo jets — and many smaller rooms for restaurants and meetings. This five-block civic center was Pei's first major project in his adopted home city of New York.

In the late 1980s, as the Chinese Communist government became more open to outside influences, Pei was able to return to China to work on several projects. The most notable was the 70-story Bank of China. The new building was located in Hong Kong, a British territory that is sched-uled to be returned to China in 1997. Ironically, the Hong Kong branch of the bank had been founded by Pei's father in 1919. At 1,100 feet, it is the tallest building outside of the United States. A model of this building sits in Pei's New York office with a cartoon cutout of the giant ape King Kong trying to figure out how to climb the bank's tower of triangles. Pei had thought this modern Western building would represent the new China on its way to democratization, but the Chinese government's 1989 massacre of anti-government demonstrators at Tiananmen Square in Beijing affected him deeply. In a rare public statement in the *New York Times*, Pei described these events as China's return to a closed society and said that these political changes would probably keep him from re-turning to China to work. He expressed dismay that his spectacular tower might come to symbolize a cruel and repressive government.

Since 1989, when Pei changed the name of his firm to Pei Cobb Freed & Partners to include the names of his partners, he has tried to reduce his

Pyramid Entrance to the Grand Louvre, 1976

role in the firm by taking on smaller projects that especially appeal to him. These "smaller" projects include a bell tower for a Buddhist temple in Japan and the Rock-'n'-Roll Hall of Fame in Cleveland, Ohio, which opened in 1995. In the Hall of Fame, he hoped that his design did justice to the "energy . . . and the spontaneity of the music." In addition, he worked on the second phase of the Louvre extension.

Pei's work has always generated some controversy, and critics continue to debate the nature of his architectural vision and the lasting value of his designs. Ultimately, each person looking at Pei's work must decide whether his imposing, geometric masterpieces—such as the East Building annex to the National Gallery, the pyramidal grand entrance to the Louvre, and the Mort—are cold and impersonal, or whether, instead, his use of glass, marble, limestone, and other materials that transform light into radiance reflect the meaning of his name: "to inscribe brightly."

MARRIAGE AND FAMILY

In 1942, Pei married Eileen Loo of China, who had been sent by her family to the United States to study at Harvard as a landscape architect. They have four children. One son, T'ing Chung, became a real-estate developer, while the other two sons, Chien Chung ("Didi") and Li Chung ("Sandi"), joined their father's firm. Their daughter, Liane, is an attorney. The Pei family residence remains in New York City. The family's country house in Katonah, New York, designed by Pei in 1952, is constructed of timber with glass skylights and is entirely surrounded by a screened porch. It highlights the interplay of sun and shadow. Pei often retreats there to work in his beloved gardens.

HONORS AND AWARDS

Arnold Brunner Award (National Institute of Arts and Letters): 1961
Medal of Honor (American Institute of Architects): 1963
Thomas Jefferson Medal in Architecture (Thomas Jefferson Memorial Foundation): 1976
Induction into American Institute of Architects: 1978
Gold Medal (American Institute of Architects): 1979
Gold Medal (American Academy and Institute of Arts and Letters): 1979
Induction into National Council on the Arts: 1980
Creative Arts Award (Brandeis University): 1981
Gold Medal of Honor for Visual Arts (National Arts Club): 1981
Gold Medal (Academie d'Architecture, France): 1981
Pritzker Architecture Prize: 1983
Medal of Liberty: 1986
Medal of the Legion of Honor (France): 1988
Praemium Imperiale (Japan Art Association): 1989
First Imperial Award for Excellence (Calbert Foundation): 1991

FURTHER READING

BOOKS

Cannell, Michael. *I.M. Pei: Mandarin of Modernism,* 1995
Contemporary Architects, 1994
Dell, Pamela. *I.M. Pei, Designer of Dreams,* 1993 (juvenile)
Encyclopedia Americana, 1995
Encyclopedia Britannica, 1995
Grolier Library of North American Biographies, 1994
Who's Who in America, 1996
Who's Who in American Art, 1995-96
Wiseman, Carter. *I.M. Pei: A Profile in American Architecture,* 1990
World Book Encyclopedia, 1996

PERIODICALS

ARTNews, Summer 1995, p.96
Current Biography Yearbook 1990
New York, Dec. 21, 1992, p.82

New York Times, Sep. 3, 1995, Section 2, p.H30
New York Times Magazine, May 20, 1979, p.24
Newsweek, Sep. 25, 1989, p.60
Time, Nov. 29, 1993, p.68
Vanity Fair, Sep. 1989, p.52

ADDRESS

Pei Cobb Freed & Partners
600 Madison Avenue
New York, NY 10022

OBITUARY

Diego Rivera 1886-1957
Mexican Artist, Muralist, and
Revolutionary
Illustrator of Revolutionary Mexico

BIRTH

Diego Rivera, whose full name is Diego Maria Concepcion
Juan Nepomuceno Estanislao de la Rivera y Barrientos
Acosta y Rodriguez, was born on December 8, 1886, in
Guanajuato, Mexico. He was the son of Maria del Pilar
Barrientos and Diego Rivera, a mine owner and school-
teacher. His ethnic background was diverse: the great-grand-

son of a Spanish nobleman, called a marquis, he was also descended from Russian, Jewish, and Mexican-Indian ancestors.

YOUTH

Rivera's interest in large-scale art murals started when he was very young. By the age of three, he was scribbling pictures on walls. So, his father built Diego's first studio: a room with blackboard walls and lots of colored chalk. Soon the blackboards were covered with big pictures of family, neighbors, and his hometown.

EDUCATION

When the family moved to Mexico City in 1892, young Diego was enrolled in an exclusive private school, the Liceo Catolico Hispano-Mexicano. After graduating with honors in 1898, Diego won a government scholarship to the San Carlos Academy of Fine Arts, where he devoted himself to classical art.

The young teenager soon heard voices of rebellion among his classmates. Like many Mexican adults, these youths opposed the one-man rule of Mexico's leader, dictator Porfirio Diaz. During his long rule, Diaz had modernized Mexico economically, but workers and farmers had suffered. Also, ordinary people had few political rights and wanted more freedom. Diego enthusiastically joined his fellow students in several protests, for which he was kicked out of school in 1902.

Thereafter, Rivera kept his art alive by painting numerous scenes of his Mexican surroundings: its houses, churches, volcanoes, Indians. But after nearly five years on his own, he longed to see the artistic riches of Europe. In 1907, at the age of 21, he sailed for Spain. There, he studied privately with distinguished teachers and showed promise of becoming a major artist.

Rivera was also an avid reader, especially of the writings of such influential thinkers as the French philosopher Voltaire, the English evolutionist Charles Darwin, the English novelist Aldous Huxley, and the German philosopher Karl Marx. The ideas of Marx were important to the development of Socialism and Communism, two economic systems based on community ownership of property. Fascinated by Europe's social atmosphere, Rivera ended his formal art instruction and toured Europe, before settling in Paris to begin his career as an artist.

CAREER HIGHLIGHTS

In 1910, Rivera left France and returned to Mexico, where he witnessed the outbreak of violent social unrest as Mexico's revolution began.

Throughout that time, from 1910 to 1920, unrest and civil war were common in Mexico. By the end of 1911, he had returned to Paris, where his works were influenced by cubism, an abstract art movement of the early 20th century in which objects were fragmented and recreated as intricate geometric forms. Rivera had his first one-man show at a Paris gallery in 1914. Interested in the technique of painting over wet plaster called "fresco," he found inspiration in Italy, where he journeyed in 1920 to see the works of Italian fresco masters Giotto and Masaccio.

REVOLUTION IN THE AIR

The years preceding 1920 were a turbulent time of revolution and world war. Mindful of Mexico's oppression, Rivera was inspired by the Russian Revolution of 1917 and its promise to liberate the working class. Rivera had Russian friends living in Paris, and he learned to speak Russian. He even had a Russian sweetheart, artist Angelina Beloff. They had a son, who died before Rivera returned to Mexico.

With his Russian friends hailing the downfall of Russia's wealthy ruling class, Rivera was stirred by news of the continuing revolution in his homeland, which eventually brought a more liberal government to Mexico. In 1921, after 14 years spent almost entirely in Europe studying art and politics, Rivera knew it was time to return to Mexico.

GOING HOME

The artist found a warm welcome in Mexico. The new government was anxious to unite the Mexican people after the revolutionary violence of the previous decade and found art a very effective tool. Rivera was immediately welcomed by a circle of revolutionary artists. He won government commissions to create art glorifying the Mexican people and their revolution.

Rivera threw himself into his new mission of portraying liberated Mexico. In his first job for the government, Rivera used all he learned in Europe and all he remembered of Mexican folk art. Called *Creation*, it is a 1,000-square-foot mural that glows in rich earth colors done in the fresco technique. The fresco shows the story of Genesis, the biblical account of creation, portrayed by men and women who look Mexican. *Creation*, his first major work at home, was very popular. His sponsor, the government, saw it as exalting Mexico's world role. Ordinary Mexicans felt good seeing Adam and Eve, the "first humans," looking like their brothers and sisters.

With the success of *Creation*, Diego Rivera became the most important artist of the Mexican Revolution. In 1923, he was chosen to create more than 100 murals for Mexico City's Ministry of Education. He also found time to create frescoes at the National Agricultural School in Chapingo.

These were hailed by a noted French art figure, Louis Gillet, as "the Sistine Chapel of the New Age." Rivera's crowning achievement for the government were the murals for the National Palace in Mexico City. In three sections, they portray ancient Mexico, the revolution, and an overview of Mexican society. True to the Rivera tradition, they glorify Mexican workers and society in a style influenced by European masters but anchored in native folk art.

Some art historians have said Rivera had a remarkable sense of timing: he was always in the right place at the right time. He had returned to Mexico just as the social reforms of political revolution were in full flower, turning walls of public buildings into huge murals that were really political posters saluting the Mexican worker. Dedicated to championing the working class, Rivera went to Russia in 1927 to dramatize the tenth anniversary of the Russian Revolution and the triumph of Communism. And in the 1930s, with the Great Depression at hand, Rivera made his first visit to the United States.

RIVERA IN AMERICA

In 1930, Rivera moved to the United States—the heartland of capitalism, an economic system that stands in direct opposition to Communism. He was eager to create murals celebrating the workers' struggle. During the next 11 years, the artist painted large and provocative murals in San Francisco, New York City, and Detroit. His first big U.S. commission, in 1931, was a mural at the California Stock Exchange Luncheon Club, a strange setting for a Mexican Marxist. Later that year, his American reputation was made in a one-man exhibition at New York City's Museum of Modern Art. One work, entitled *Frozen Assets*, outraged some critics who saw it as an attack on the city's wealth. Diego Rivera was stirring up trouble, and there was more to come.

DETROIT INDUSTRY

Edsel Ford, the son of U.S. automobile pioneer Henry Ford, hired Rivera in 1932 to do enormous murals at the Detroit Institute of Arts dramatizing the automobile industry. Art critics used the word "magnificent" to describe the murals. They portrayed the evolution of humankind from the Garden of Eden to the 20th century, culminating in massive machinery run by dedicated workers. Rivera was proud of this *Detroit Industry* series, and Edsel Ford felt he had gotten his money's worth. Then someone made a discovery. One scene showed a baby being vaccinated—innocent enough, until it was noted that the infant was held by a female nurse and was vaccinated by a male doctor. Before them were the animals from which the vaccine was made. Behind them were three scientists in white coats making tests. It instantly inflamed various Christian groups who saw it as a mockery of the Holy Family—Jesus, Mary, and Joseph—and

Detroit Industry, north wall, vaccination panel, 1932-33

the three Wise Men. Lured as much by the controversy as the oversized art, huge crowds thronged the Detroit Institute of Arts to see what this man from Mexico was up to. Most visitors liked what they saw. Edsel Ford ruled that the murals would remain, and the controversy fizzled. But another controversy was already brewing.

MAN AT THE CROSSROADS

In 1933, Rivera found an even bigger forum: Radio City Music Hall in New York City's Rockefeller Center. Visited by millions of moviegoers and tourists every year, Radio City was called the "Showplace of the Nation," the crown in the Rockefeller family's New York City empire. Brushes in hand, Rivera quickly got to work on an enormous mural he called *Man at the Crossroads.* In the center was the figure of Man and on either side were large panels showing the events of American life. One scene was a May Day demonstration of marching workers. As the mural neared completion, it became clear that the labor leader in the scene looked remarkably like Vladimir Ilich Lenin, the Russian revolutionary and founding father of the Soviet Union. (Years later, a letter was discovered that suggested that including Lenin was not Rivera's idea, but that of Abby Aldrich Rockefeller, the wife of John D. Rockefeller, Jr.)

The response to Lenin's portrait was overwhelming. There were angry newspaper and radio editorials and noisy demonstrations. Nelson Rockefeller, who later became the governor of New York, politely ordered Rivera to paint Lenin out. Rivera refused, but as a compromise, he offered to add a likeness of Abraham Lincoln to the painting. Unmoved, Rockefeller paid Rivera his full $21,500 fee and ordered the mural removed. Some said his plan was to return it to Rivera, but workmen chipped out the stone and destroyed it. Now there was another outcry, this time against the Rockefellers for destroying fine art. Further controversy ensued when a New York City newspaper article claimed that Communist artists thought Rivera was "pulling his punches" because he was paid by the rich Rockefellers. Rivera's supporters said that he was going to prove he was not afraid of any capitalist, no matter how rich. In any event, Diego Rivera found the controversy he desired, and he continued to let his art make his social statements. Snubbed by the rich, he painted murals for the New Workers School in New York, using heroic portraits of American patriots Abraham Lincoln, Benjamin Franklin, and Thomas Paine, and uncomplimentary portraits of capitalist millionaires J. P. Morgan and the Rockefellers.

LATER CAREER

Returning to Mexico, Rivera won permission to recreate the Radio City mural in the Palace of Fine Arts in Mexico City. In his later years, he continued turning out impressive fresco murals throughout Mexico and the United States, mostly in colleges, universities, and luxury hotels. His later murals included those for the Cardiological Institute of Mexico in 1943 and for a hotel in Mexico City in 1948. He was working on murals in Mexico City's National Palace, showing the history of Mexico, when he died on November 25, 1957.

LEGACY

Some critics dismiss Diego Rivera as a propagandist, someone who uses his work to advance economic, political, or social programs. Others have said that if he was a propagandist, he was a magnificent one. Rivera himself, referring to the masterworks of the past, called all art propaganda of a kind.

Jere Abbott, former associate director of the Museum of Modern Art said, "Since the Renaissance no one has perhaps equaled Diego in the mastery of fresco painting. . . . [Here one feels] the vitality of a great artist who feels keenly the problems of his native Mexico." Critic Mark Stevens, writing in *Newsweek,* saw Rivera's murals as closer in spirit to art of the Middle Ages than to modern art: "Like medieval and renaissance frescoes, they claim to fix man's place in the universe. . . . He was born, like earlier artists, into a largely preliterate society rich in myth. . . . [His work] has an innocence found almost nowhere else in modern art." Rivera said himself of his work, "For me, painting and life are one."

MARRIAGE AND FAMILY

In 1929, when he was 43, Rivera married Frida Kahlo, herself a noted artist. They divorced in 1939 yet remarried the year after. They lived in a Mexico City suburb in a double house linked by a bridge. Diego lived in the "Big House" with a two-story studio, while Frida lived in the "Little House," until his death in 1957.

SELECTED WRITINGS

Portrait of America, 1934
Portrait of Mexico, 1937

FURTHER READING

BOOKS

Cockcroft, James D. *Diego Rivera,* 1989 (juvenile)
Detroit Institute of Arts. *Diego Rivera: A Retrospective,* 1986
Encyclopedia Americana, 1995
Encyclopedia Britannica, 1995
Gleiter, Jan. *Diego Rivera,* 1989
Museum of Modern Art. *Diego Rivera,* 1931
Neimark, Anne E. *Diego Rivera: Artist of the People,* 1992 (juvenile)
Pan American Union. *Diego Rivera,* 1947
Who Was Who, Vol. III
Wolfe, Bertram D. *Diego Rivera,* 1939
World Book Encyclopedia, 1996

PERIODICALS

Americas, Mar./Apr. 1992, p.26
Current Biography Yearbook 1948; 1958 (obituary)
New York Times, Nov. 25, 1957, p.1; Aug. 28, 1988, Section 2, p.29
Newsweek, Mar. 10, 1986, p.72
People, July 7, 1986, p.16
Smithsonian, Feb. 1986, p.36
USA Today Magazine, Feb. 1986, p.36

OBITUARY

Norman Rockwell   1894-1978
American Artist
Renowned for His Cover Illustrations for
the *Saturday Evening Post*

BIRTH

Norman Percevel Rockwell was born on February 3, 1894, in
the back bedroom of a small apartment in New York City.
He was the second son of J. Waring Rockwell, who managed
the New York office of a textile firm, and Nancy Hill
Rockwell, daughter of William Hill, an amateur English portrait and landscape painter who came from England to

America after the American Civil War. Norman Rockwell was named after an English ancestor on his mother's side of the family, Sir Norman Percevel, who is credited with having kicked Guy Fawkes down the stairs of the Tower of London after Fawkes tried to blow up the Houses of Parliament in the 16th century. Rockwell hated his middle name—he dreaded being nicknamed "Percy"—and stopped using it completely as soon as he left home. He had one brother, Jarvis, who was a year and a half older.

YOUTH

Norman Rockwell's early years were spent living and going to school in a series of New York City neighborhoods as the family moved often in trying to improve its living conditions. Waring Rockwell was a devoted but very modestly paid employee of George Wood, Sons, and Company, where he had begun his career as a lowly office boy. The family never lacked food, clothing, or other necessities, but Norman was embarrassed by his family's worn furniture and his own lack of cash. His father was handsome, dignified, and stern. Although he was distant with his two sons, treating them more like adults than children, he was devoted to his wife, who was often ill. Norman never felt close to either of his parents.

On those Sunday evenings when Mrs. Rockwell was too sick to attend church, the family would gather in the parlor to sing hymns together. Sometimes on weekday evenings, after the boys had finished their homework, Mr. Rockwell would read from the novels of Charles Dickens. The family would sit around the dining-room table and Norman's head would be bent over a sheet of paper, a pencil clutched in his hand as he struggled to draw pictures of the characters in the novels. He would draw and erase, draw and erase, asking his father to repeat the description of Mr. Pickwick, or Oliver Twist, or Uriah Heep again and again. Dickens's writing made a strong impression on him and stimulated his curiosity about the world.

Another family activity on summer evenings was to catch a ride on the trolley for a breath of fresh air. For a fare of ten cents per person, you could ride from the Battery at the south end of Manhattan north to the Bronx and back. Norman and Jarvis always sat in the seat directly behind the motorman so they could watch him steer the trolley and work the hand brake. As they traveled further into the outskirts of the city, the stops became fewer and fewer, and the trolley would pick up speed. The two boys were thrilled at the possibility that the trolley might take a curve too fast and jump the track. At the end of the line, where the motorman and conductor turned the car around, the trolley company provided a small park. Passengers could get off and sit on benches among the trees to enjoy the country scenery. The Rockwells would pack a picnic supper and spread a tablecloth on the grass for their evening meal. Then they would catch the last trolley back into the city.

EARLY MEMORIES

Even as a child, Norman Rockwell already preferred the open, green countryside to the city. He saw life in the city as ugly, crowded, dirty, and full of drunks and thieves. Until he was nine or ten years old, his family spent a few weeks every summer at farms in the country. Far from being fancy resorts, these farms offered their boarders plenty of fresh air and plain food at a reasonable cost. While the grown-ups played croquet or sat in rocking chairs on a wide front porch, Norman and Jarvis were free to explore. They helped with the milking, fished, swam in creeks and farm ponds, and fell off horses and out of haylofts like real country boys. These glorious summers spent in the country left Rockwell with many happy memories that stayed with him, appearing often in his later paintings. Years later, in describing what influenced him to paint the way he did, Rockwell mentioned his happy, carefree summers as a boy and his love of what he saw as a good life in the country. "The view of life I communicate in my pictures excludes the sordid and ugly. I paint life as I would like it to be." Although others called it an idealized view of life, Rockwell said, "I guess I have a bad case of the American nostalgia for the clean, simple country life as opposed to the complicated world of the city."

CHOOSING A CAREER

Norman Rockwell always wanted to be an artist and illustrator. One of his earliest memories of enjoying art dated to when he was about six and drew ships on cardboard for his brother and another boy to cut out. The more he drew, the more he liked to draw. Eventually, he did not want to do anything else. At first, though, he saw his talent as just something he had, "like a bag of lemon drops." His brother Jarvis could leap over three orange crates, another boy could wiggle his ears, and Norman could draw. Later, however, he would cling to his drawing as the thing that gave him his identity.

EDUCATION

When Rockwell was 10 years old, the family moved to a house in Mamaroneck, New York, that was far out of the city on the road to Connecticut—a location that was almost rural then. At this time, he began to be aware of his appearance and his standing among his school-mates. A skinny, pigeon-toed boy with narrow shoulders and a promi-nent Adam's apple, he was fitted with bulky, corrective shoes that only increased his awkwardness. His mother called him "Snow-in-the-Face" because of his pale complexion. His classmates called him "Mooney"—a nickname he hated—when he received his round, rimless glasses at age 12. Rockwell was terrible at sports and felt inferior to his brother, who was the best athlete in school. Norman began to withdraw into his drawing in order to forget his physical shortcomings.

In the classroom, when Rockwell was supposed to be reading his textbooks, he was most often doodling in the margins instead. Because of this, his grades were never good. Even in art he had barely passing grades throughout elementary school. Fortunately, his eighth-grade teacher, Julia M. Smith, recognized his ability and encouraged him to draw for the class. She asked him to draw Christmas pictures on the blackboard in colored chalks. During history lessons, he drew soldiers and covered wagons, and in science, he drew animals. Smith was the first adult to show public approval of his talent.

During his first year at Mamaroneck High School in 1908, Rockwell began to use the money he was earning doing odd jobs to pay for art classes on Saturdays at the Chase School of Fine and Applied Art in New York City. It was a two-hour commute each way. In November, the principal of Mamaroneck High School gave him permission to take every Wednesday off so that he could attend classes twice a week at Chase. That next summer, Rockwell began delivering mail to the wealthy people who resided in the summer homes on the edge of town. He picked up the mail at the post office at 5:30 each morning and rode his bicycle from house to house, for which he earned about $2.50 per day. One of his subscribers, Mrs. James Constable, the widow of a department-store founder, gave him his first paid job as an artist when she commissioned him to paint four Christmas cards.

In the middle of his sophomore year, Rockwell quit high school to become a full-time art student, this time at the National Academy of Design in New York City. For two months, he spent eight hours a day, six days a week, making charcoal drawings from battered plaster statues of various gods, goddesses, and athletes. Finally, he was allowed to join the life drawing class, where he could work from nude models. After several months, however, he decided to change schools again. He found the Academy too stiff and scholarly and especially disliked the lack of classes in illustration. Other students told him about the Art Students League in Manhattan, and when he discovered that one of its founders was his idol—the great American illustrator Howard Pyle—Norman made up his mind to switch.

On his first day at the Art Students League, a coin toss put him in the life drawing class taught by George Bridgeman, who became his favorite teacher. Rockwell would later look back on this time and say that Bridgeman may not have taught him everything he knew, but "perhaps the most important part of what I know." Bridgeman was a short, stocky man in rumpled clothes who smoked big black cigars and seldom came to class sober. An excellent draftsman, he insisted that the students learn about the human skeletal and muscular systems. He sometimes drew directly on the model's skin with red chalk to illustrate exactly how a particular muscle attached to a particular bone. In his second year there, Rockwell received the job of monitor for Bridgeman's class, which meant that his tuition was free in exchange for scheduling the models and keeping order in the classroom.

Rockwell also took a class in illustration with Thomas Fogarty, an equally dedicated teacher. Fogarty was a small, bird-like man, very neat and polite, who demanded that the students' drawings be faithful to the story in every detail. From him, Rockwell learned to search for authentic costumes, props, and settings. A practicing professional illustrator, Fogarty would sometimes turn assignments over to the class and also helped Rockwell get a variety of small illustrating jobs to help pay his expenses. In 1911, Fogarty sent Rockwell to his first real job.

CAREER HIGHLIGHTS

Rockwell's first professional assignment was for the publishing firm McBride, Nast, and Company, illustrating a children's book called *Tell-Me-Why Stories*. His next project was a volume on camping written by Edward Cave, the editor of the Boy Scouts magazine, *Boys' Life*. Cave liked Rockwell's work and began to give him stories to illustrate for *Boys' Life*, eventually awarding him his first real job as art director of the magazine. Rockwell did the cover and one set of illustrations for each issue. He also developed a successful freelance career doing illustrations for such young people's magazines as *St. Nicholas, The Youth's Companion,* and *The American Boy*. Rockwell had a long and happy relationship with the Scouts. Later in his career, he would make time each year from 1926 to 1976 to do a painting for the Boy Scouts of America calendar. In gratitude, the Scouts presented him with an award for outstanding service to the Boy Scouts.

SATURDAY EVENING POST

By the time Rockwell moved to New Rochelle, New York, at age 21, one of his greatest ambitions was to do a cover for the *Saturday Evening Post*. Any illustrator who landed a *Post* cover was considered a success, and he desperately wanted to be among that crowd. He was sharing a studio with the cartoonist Clyde Forsythe, who finally persuaded him to submit his work. Rockwell's first cover for the *Saturday Evening Post* appeared on May 20, 1916. It showed a frowning, dressed-up boy pushing a baby carriage past two smirking friends in play clothes on their way to play baseball.

Over the next 47 years, he created 321 covers for the magazine. His work for the *Post* would make him perhaps the most widely recognized artist in America. The public loved his subject matter, which often featured ordinary Americans in familiar family settings: at parades and picnics, at home and at work. Rockwell's covers for the *Post* showed the major events in American history, from World Wars I and II to the integration of African-American children into previously all-white schools. His illustrations became noted for their careful, realistic details, which made them seem almost like photographs. According to Edwin McDowell in the *New York Times*, "a typical Rockwell cover tended to evoke emotions of sentiment, reverence, or poignancy: a family gathered in thanksgiving around a holiday table; ample Pickwickian gentlemen singing Christmas carols; freckled boys, barefoot and in tattered overalls, carrying makeshift fishing poles; the kindly doctor preparing to inoculate a wide-eyed child's bare bottom; a run-away boy at a lunch counter confiding in an understanding policeman; a tomboy with a black eye in he doctor's waiting room or shy young couples bathed in the innocence of new love."

When the United States entered World War I in 1917, Rockwell tried to enlist in the U.S. Navy, but he was rejected because he was 17 pounds underweight. After stuffing himself with bananas, doughnuts, and water, he managed to gain enough weight to be accepted. However, he spent his entire time in the service in the Charleston navy yard, where he worked on a navy newspaper and painted portraits of admirals. He was also allowed to continue doing covers for the *Post*. After the war, he returned to New Rochelle.

During the 1920s, he traveled to South America and to Europe, where for the first time he studied the paintings of such famous artists as Rembrandt and Vermeer. Rockwell became concerned that the art world was passing him by when he encountered the new styles of cubism and abstract color. Although he tried to adapt his style to the new trends, the *Post* asked him to go back to his old way of painting.

In the 1930s and 1940s, Rockwell did some of his finest work, and his popularity soared. In the 1930s, he first started to use photographs of his posed models, rather than painting the live models themselves. Rockwell had a large collection of authentic period costumes and props. He would dress his models in costumes, take photographs of scenes in which he arranged the models, and then create his painting from the photographs. He was always working under a deadline and said that the photographs saved him a lot of time. But he received a lot of criticism for that practice throughout his career, because critics believed that only live models provided sufficient realism for art. Around 1935, he did the illustrations for new editions of Mark Twain's *Tom Sawyer* and *Huckleberry Finn*, traveling to Hannibal, Missouri, to get the flavor of Twain's stories. He also illustrated a biography of novelist Louisa May Alcott. In 1939, he moved to Arlington, Vermont, and his work began to focus even more on small-town American life.

THE FOUR FREEDOMS

When World War II arrived, Rockwell wanted to do something big to help the war effort. He woke up in the middle of the night on July 16, 1942, with the idea of illustrating the concept of the Four Freedoms—Freedom Of Speech, Freedom From Fear, Freedom Of Worship, and Freedom From Want—as they had been described by President Franklin D. Roosevelt in his annual message to Congress. Rockwell soon began work on four paintings on these themes. As John Russell explained in the *New York Times*, "When Franklin D. Roosevelt defined the four essential freedoms in his annual message to the Congress on January 6, 1941, Norman Rockwell knew that something fundamental was at stake, and he put that speech into images that would strike home across the boundaries of language." *Freedom Of Speech* showed a plainly dressed man speaking at a New England town meeting, while *Freedom From Fear* pictured a mother and father adjusting the blankets over their peacefully sleeping children. In *Freedom Of Worship* an old couple prays, and in *Freedom From Want* a large, happy family prepares to eat the Thanksgiving turkey. Rockwell took his sketches to Washington, D.C., to offer them to the government, but no one was interested. On the train back, he decided to stop in Philadelphia at the offices of the *Post* and see if his luck would change. In 1943, the *Post* not only published this set of four soon-to-be-famous paintings, but enlisted the government's interest as well. The paintings toured the country in an exhibition sponsored by the *Post* and the U.S. Treasury Department to sell war bonds. The tour raised more than $130 million to support the war effort. The government printed several million copies of the paintings and distributed them around the world.

Rockwell's unprecedented triumph that year was balanced by a great tragedy. His studio in Arlington burned to the ground, the fire perhaps started by his ever-present pipe. He lost a number of paintings and his entire collection of authentic period costumes and props.

THE STOCKBRIDGE YEARS

During the last part of his life Rockwell was America's most popular artist, but he also underwent important career and personal changes. For

Freedom From Want, 1943

the Thanksgiving 1951 issue, Rockwell painted his most famous *Post* cover. It showed a grandmother and grandson saying grace over a simple meal in a modest restaurant near a railroad station as the other customers look on. In 1952, he painted a portrait of President Dwight D. Eisenhower. The following year, Rockwell moved to Stockbridge, Massachusetts, where he would remain until his death in 1978. He published an autobiography, *My Adventures as an Illustrator,* written and illustrated with his son Thomas Rockwell, in 1960. Also in that year, he painted portraits of both of the presidential candidates, Senator John F. Kennedy and Vice President Richard M. Nixon. During the 1960s, Rockwell painted a number of portraits of famous politicians and their wives, including President Lyndon B. Johnson and his wife, Lady Bird.

After more than 45 years, Rockwell and the *Post* ended their relationship in 1963. Guided by new management and trying to boost its circulation, the *Post* decided to switch to photographs on the cover. Rockwell then began doing illustrations for *Look* magazine, where his subjects changed radically. At *Look*, he covered the civil-rights movement, President Johnson's "war on poverty," protest marches, and the Peace Corps. In 1965, he began a series on the American space program, which eventually included a painting of man's first steps on the moon. In 1968, Rockwell had his first one-man show in New York City when the Bernard Dannenberg Gallery on Madison Avenue exhibited 50 of his oil paintings. The artist was thrilled, but the art critics thought his work was too sentimental for the more realistic art of the 20th century. Rockwell defended the often whimsical, too-good-to-be-true subjects of his paintings by saying, "I paint what I do the way I do because that's how I feel about things."

In the 1970s, Rockwell began to branch out into other media. He made more than 80 pieces of art for a Franklin Mint series of collectibles, which was very popular. He also created designs for a series of 12 silver medals, called the "Spirit of Scouting," for the Boy Scouts. In 1976, Rockwell placed his Stockbridge studio and all its contents in trust to the Norman Rockwell Museum in Stockbridge. One year later he received the Presidential Medal of Freedom. Rockwell died at his home in Stockbridge on November 8, 1978, at the age of 84.

In 1993, the Norman Rockwell Museum, which houses the largest collection of Rockwell art in the world, was moved to its current home with the opening of a new and larger building located a few miles outside of Stockbridge. Rockwell's studio was also moved to that site.

LEGACY

Rockwell's idealized view of American life has come in for its fair share of criticism. Many have disagreed with his limited and unrealistic depiction of society, which excluded all minorities and which escaped all problems. Scholars have criticized his lack of subtlety, nuance, and depth, saying that his work will not live on in the history of art. Rockwell acknowledged that his illustrations did not always reflect real life, yet he defended them just the same. "Maybe I grew up and found the world wasn't the perfectly pleasant place I had thought it to be. I unconsciously decided that if it wasn't an ideal world, it should be, and so painted only the ideal aspects of it, pictures in which there were no drunken fathers, or self-centered mothers, in which on the contrary, there were only foxy Grandpas who played baseball with the kids, and boys fished from logs and got up circuses in the backyard. If there were problems, they were humorous problems." For that vision of America, and for the feelings of nostalgia and sentimental warmth that it engendered, Rockwell has been revered by millions of America.

MARRIAGE AND FAMILY

Norman Rockwell was married three times. He was first married in 1916 to Irene O'Connor, a young schoolteacher he met in the New Rochelle boardinghouse where they both lived. That marriage ended in divorce in 1928. His second marriage was to Mary Rhoads Barstow, a schoolteacher who he met on a vacation trip to California and married in 1930. Norman and Mary had three sons — Jarvis, Thomas, and Peter. Mary died in 1959 of a heart attack. Two years later, Rockwell married Mary (Molly) L. Punderson, a retired schoolteacher, in 1961.

SELECTED WRITINGS

My Adventures as an Illustrator, 1960 (with Thomas Rockwell)
How I Make a Picture, 1979

HONORS AND AWARDS

Silver Buffalo Award (Boy Scouts of America): 1939
Presidential Medal of Freedom: 1977

FURTHER READING

BOOKS

Buechner, Thomas S. *Norman Rockwell: Artist and Illustrator,* 1970
Encyclopedia Americana, 1995
Encyclopedia Britannica, 1995
Meyer, Susan E. *Norman Rockwell's World War II: Impressions from the Homefront,* 1991
Norman Rockwell Museum. *Norman Rockwell: A Centennial Celebration,* 1993
Rockwell, Norman, and Thomas Rockwell. *My Adventures as an Illustrator,* 1960
Stoltz, Donald. *The Advertising World of Norman Rockwell,* 1985
Walton, Donald. *A Rockwell Portrait: An Intimate Biography,* 1978
Who Was Who, Vol. VII
World Book Encyclopedia, 1996

PERIODICALS

Boston Globe, Apr. 2, 1993, p.85
Cobblestone, Dec. 1989 (entire issue)
Current Biography Yearbook 1945; 1979 (obituary)
Economist, Dec. 25, 1993-Jan. 7, 1994, p.37
New York Times, Nov. 10, 1978, pp.A1 and A29; June 13, 1993, p.1
Newsweek, Apr. 12, 1993, p.58
Saturday Evening Post, Jan. 1979, p.36 (and other articles); May/June 1994
   (Norman Rockwell Anniversary Issue); May/June 1995, p.60
Smithsonian, July 1994, p.88
Time, Nov. 20, 1978, p.110
U.S. News and World Report, Feb. 7, 1994, p.10

VIDEOCASSETTES

Norman Rockwell: An American Portrait, 1987
Norman Rockwell's World, 1987

OBITUARY

Andy Warhol   1928?-1987
American Painter, Sculptor, Silk-Screen
Artist, and Filmmaker
One of the Founders of Pop Art

BIRTH

Andy Warhol was born Andrew Warhola. His birth date and
place of birth are unknown, but most sources believe the date
was August 6, 1928. He was probably born in Pittsburgh,
Pennsylvania, but he at times indicated that he was born in
Philadelphia or McKeesport, Pennsylvania. One of three children of Czech immigrants Ondrej and Julia Warhola, Andy
Warhol had two brothers, John and Paul Warhola.

YOUTH

Information about Warhol's early life is sketchy and available primarily from his own statements. Since he sometimes provided conflicting facts and dates, accounts of these early years differ. Some facts appear to be clear, however. Warhol had a difficult childhood, growing up in poverty while trying to deal with emotional strains. He later reported that he had three nervous breakdowns before he was 11, and he contracted a childhood disease that turned his skin chalky white and made his hair fall out.

Warhol's father, a coal miner and steel worker in McKeesport, near Pittsburgh, died in 1942 when Andy was 14, leaving the family in poverty. Warhol had to sell vegetables on the street to earn money. When he came home at night, his mother comforted him by reading "Dick Tracy" comic strips. As a teenager, Warhol got a summer job at a department store. Given his artistic temperament, it turned his thoughts to fashion design and drawing.

EDUCATION

Little is known about Warhol's secondary school career. After finishing high school, he scraped up enough money to enroll in the Carnegie Institute of Technology (now called Carnegie-Mellon University) in Pittsburgh. He graduated in 1949 with a bachelor of arts degree in pictorial design and headed for New York City to seek his fortune. It did not take him long to find it.

FIRST JOBS

One of Warhol's biggest breaks came as the result of a rather humiliating experience. After waiting hours to see an important editor at the fashion magazine *Harper's Bazaar*, Warhol opened his paper bag of sketches and a cockroach ran out. The editor, apparently moved by Warhol's pitiful circumstances, gave him an assignment. Before the end of 1949, Andy Warhol was a busy freelance artist, designing newspaper advertising for Fifth Avenue department stores and drawing illustrations for fashion magazines. He worked for Tiffany's, Bonwit Teller's, *Vogue*, and *Glamour*, among others, and soon rose to the top rank among New York commercial artists. In 1957 he won an award for a shoe advertisement, and in 1961 his large paintings of Dick Tracy comic strips were first used in a department store display.

But Warhol was unsatisfied with commercial success. He also hoped to create fine art and wondered if his work would ever appear in museums. He started collecting works of contemporary artists, found friends in the New York art world, and began exhibiting his original drawings in 1956. Critics said he was a young artist of exceptional talent, but that his skills needed development.

CAREER HIGHLIGHTS

Andy Warhol did what few American artists have done: he became famous overnight. The desire for fame was a driving force in his life. To help achieve recognition he fashioned a special look: he dyed his shaggy hair silver and wore black leather clothing. It made him look odd, but his appearance was unforgettable. As an artist and a public personality he won wealth, popularity among famous people, and a great deal of attention in newspapers and on television. Little by little, he was accepted as an artist by art critics and the general public.

CREATOR OF POP ART

Warhol had a unique way of looking at the world. He believed that the ordinary things we see on television or read in the daily newspapers form a type of fine art. He proved it when he burst into national prominence in 1962 with the exhibition of a single, striking painting: *Campbell's Soup Can*. Overnight, the picture of the ordinary red-and-white can, familiar to millions of Americans, became a symbol of a new movement: "Pop Art." With Andy Warhol as its leader, Pop Art attracted a young audience with its revolutionary theme: art is everywhere, even in everyday life. For his subjects, Warhol chose soup cans, Brillo soap-pad boxes, and Coca-Cola bottles. "What's great about this country," Warhol once said, "is that America started the tradition where the richest consumers buy essentially the same things as the poorest." He also thought that America was built on "harsh, impersonal products and brash materialistic objects" that were "practical but impermanent symbols."

Warhol's technique was as unusual as his style. After his first paintings, he turned to silk-screening, in which several stencils of the same image are layered on top of each other, one after another, to create multi-colored prints. This technique produced almost one-dimensional prints on canvas, which made his work appear impersonal and mass-produced. "Painting a soup can is not in itself a radical act," art critic Robert Hughes explained in 1971. "But what was radical in Warhol was that he adapted the means of production of soup cans to the way he produced paintings, turning them out en masse—consumer art mimicking the process as well as the look of consumer culture." In this way, both the subject of Warhol's early works as well as their technique became a powerful critique of the depersonalization and mechanization of the increasingly commercialized culture in America. In his book *The Philosophy of Andy Warhol (From A to B and Back Again)*, Warhol reinforced this idea that art and commerce were inextricably linked. There, he explained his philosophy of art: "Being good in business is the most fascinating kind of art. Making money is art and working is art and good business is the best art."

After consumer items, Warhol's next subjects were celebrities—whom he saw as another type of product. After all, he reasoned, an individual like Marilyn Monroe or Elvis Presley or Elizabeth Taylor is just another product that is advertised, promoted, and delivered to ordinary people, like a bar of soap. Isn't a famous face, like a soup can, transmitted millions of times in newspapers and over television? So what could be more logical than to create pop art in repetitions? Such was the logic of Warhol, who filled a canvas with 100 soup cans, and another canvas with a dozen Marilyn Monroes. These pictures looked like sheets of postage stamps—the same flat image over and over. But each had its own distinct color scheme—black and white, pink, pale red, or bright red. He was particularly fascinated with Marilyn Monroe, the legendary film star and sex symbol who committed suicide in 1962. Numerous Warhol series paintings in the 1960s feature her as the subject.

There was also a tragic side to Warhol's work. His early works included horrible pictures of fatal automobile crashes and electric chairs. There was also *16 Jackies* (1964), showing the first lady, Jacqueline Kennedy (Onassis), before and after the assassination of her husband, President John F. Kennedy, in 1963.

Warhol's personal and professional style was cool and distant. "I don't want to get involved in other people's lives," he once said. "I don't want to get too close." A friend said that if she tried to touch him, he would actually shrink away. He had the same attitude toward creating art. His style avoided emotion and seriousness and replaced them with cartoon-like images of everyday objects.

THE FACTORY

Warhol's studio was a Manhattan building he called "The Factory," where mass-produced art was big business. Using silk-screen techniques, Warhol made many copies of his best-known works. Over time, The Factory became not merely a "machine" for producing artworks, but the site for establishing the Warhol style in other media. In the mid-1960s, he brought together there the rock music group Velvet Underground, one of the early influences on punk music. In 1969, he started *Interview* magazine, a mix of art, show business, and celebrity news. Its page-one slogan has been quoted by millions: "In the future, everyone will be famous for 15 minutes."

Warhol also made movies at The Factory, but his films were totally unlike those made in Hollywood. Experimental in approach, many were long and deliberately boring, devoid of plot and action. In his 1965 film *Empire* (1965), for example, a stationary camera focuses on the Empire State Building for eight hours. Absolutely nothing happens, except the

The Twenty Marilyns, 1962

sun changes position and clouds move. His 1966 film *The Chelsea Girls*, a seven-hour peek into hotel rooms, featured original techniques by focusing two projectors on a divided screen. His films drew mixed reviews. Some critics loved the originality of Warhol's approach, while others thought these films had no value.

Over time, The Factory became more than just an artist's studio. It became a celebrity gathering place, one to which gossip columnists and celebrity photographers flocked. The Factory attracted the unconventional, the avant-garde, and the famous from all areas — artists, photographers, actors, and musicians. But it also enticed all sorts of hangers-on who were interested in experimenting with drugs and sex. Soon, Warhol and his admirers were seen at every "in" party. Warhol's outrageous public image became an important element of his art.

At the peak of his career, in 1968, Warhol was shot and seriously wounded by Valerie Solanis, an aspiring actress associated with The Factory who was known to hate all men, and Warhol in particular. She was later found to be mentally incompetent and was committed to a mental hospital. Warhol was near death for weeks, and his health and art never fully recovered. From then on, his popularity faded. After that, he began doing "commissioned portraits," charging large fees for paintings of such famous people as President Jimmy Carter, actresses Ingrid Bergman and Grace Kelly, and newscaster Maria Shriver. The Factory became a meeting place for the rich and glamorous international high-society, and Warhol was accused of snobbism.

In the years after he was shot, Warhol also tried to regain his position as a leader of the American art world. He often portrayed subjects that were disturbing to wealthy art patrons, such as violent homosexuality and German Nazi themes. He branched out into television, creating advertising and hosting a cable-TV show. Andy Warhol's life ended unexpectedly on February 22, 1987, in New York City. Hours after undergoing gall-bladder surgery, he died of heart failure. Warhol left an estate worth about $15 million, most of it to a foundation for the visual arts. Two years before he died, Warhol had said he wanted his tombstone blank. "Well, actually, I'd like it to say 'figment'."

LEGACY

Warhol was a profoundly enigmatic artist, as Franz Erhard Walther explained in *Contemporary Artists*. "At a time when enigma is one of the most sought after of aesthetic virtues, Andy Warhol has achieved the difficult feat of remaining the most enigmatic artist of all. Since he first became known at the beginning of the Pop Art boom in the early 1960s, critics and public have argued about him, dismissed him, reinstated him again, endlessly questioned him, and in the absence of an useful statement by the artist himself, declared themselves baffled by the bland success of his art."

To this day, Warhol remains a puzzle. Few people are really certain what he stood for, or if, in fact, he stood for anything. He offered no clues, saying, "If you want to know all about Andy Warhol, just look at the surface of my paintings and films and me, and there I am. There's nothing behind it." Some have said this means that Warhol admitted to being shallow and that he was obsessed with fame. Recently, however, critics have judged more him positively, and some say that Warhol's life and work made a very bold and challenging statement: that the United States is too violent and too commercialized, and that the country's obsession with mass-produced goods creates a mass-produced culture. In other words, the shallowness of Warhol's art is a reflection of the shallowness of American culture.

After Warhol's death, Robert Hughes looked back on his contribution to the art world, commenting in *Time* magazine: "Absurd though these pictures looked at first, Warhol's fixation on repetition and glut emerged as the most powerful statement ever made by an American artist on the subject of a consumer economy." As Douglas C. McGill of the *New York Times* explained following his death, "Warhol's keenest talents were for attracting publicity, for uttering the unforgettable quote, and for finding the single visual image that would most shock and endure. That his art could attract and maintain the public interest made him among the most influential and widely emulated artists of his time."

FILMS

Harlot, 1964
Empire, 1965
The Velvet Underground, 1966
The Chelsea Girls, 1966
International Velvet, 1967
Blue Movie, 1969
Andy Warhol's Dracula, 1974
Andy Warhol's Frankenstein, 1974
Andy Warhol's Bad, 1977

WRITINGS

The Philosophy of Andrew Warhol (From A to B and Back Again), 1975
POPism: The Warhol 60s, 1980 (with Pat Hackett)
Andy Warhol in His Own Words, 1991

HONORS AND AWARDS

Art Directors Club Award: 1956, 1957, for distinctive merit
Art Directors Club Medal: 1957, for advertising layouts
Film Culture Award: 1964
Los Angeles Film Festival Award: 1964

FURTHER READING

BOOKS

Bockris, Victor. *The Life and Death of Andy Warhol,* 1989
Bourdon, David. *Warhol,* 1989
Colacello, Bob. *Holy Terror: Andy Warhol Close Up,* 1990
Contemporary Artists, 1996
Crone, Rainer. *Andy Warhol,* 1970
Encyclopedia Americana, 1995
Encyclopedia Britannica, 1995
Ratcliff, Carter. *Andy Warhol,* 1983
Who Was Who, Vol. IX
World Book Encyclopedia, 1996

PERIODICALS

Art in America, May 1987, p.129
ARTnews, May 1987, p.128
Atlantic, Aug. 1989, p.73
Current Biography Yearbook 1986; 1987 (obituary)
Life, Dec. 1989, p.84
New Republic, Mar. 27, 1989, p.26
New York, Mar. 9, 1987, p.38
New York Times, Feb. 23, 1987, p.A1
New Yorker, Apr. 27, 1987, p.27; Apr. 10, 1989, p.109
Newsweek, Mar. 9, 1987, p.64
Rolling Stone, Apr. 9, 1987, p.31
Smithsonian, Feb. 1989, p.11
Time, Mar. 9, 1987, p.90

OBITUARY

Frank Lloyd Wright   1869-1959
American Architect
Considered the Greatest American
Architect

BIRTH

Frank Lloyd Wright was born on June 8, 1869, in Richland
Center, Wisconsin, to Anna (Lloyd-Jones) Wright and
William Russell Cary Wright. His mother, a schoolteacher,
shared her love of architecture with Frank even before he
was born, decorating his nursery with pictures of old
English cathedrals and telling everyone that he would grow

up to be an architect. His father, who had studied medicine, law, religion, and music, was working as a Baptist minister when Frank was born. Frank had two younger sisters, Mary Jane (Jennie) and Maginel.

YOUTH

From the age of 3, Wright lived in various towns in New England, including Pawtucket, Rhode Island, and Weymouth, Massachusetts, where his father was the pastor of small churches. Around 1880, the family moved to Madison, Wisconsin, near the Lloyd-Jones family. Of Welsh descent, they were independent, strong, and courageous people who led their daily lives as Unitarians with the awareness of the Divine Presence.

Wright was solitary and referred to himself as a dreamer. He loved reading, and he would listen to music so intently that he would forget to eat. His mother, concerned about his withdrawn nature, sent him to spend his summers working on the Lloyd-Jones's farm 40 miles away. There, Wright became the favorite of the Lloyd-Jones family, and they influenced him greatly. Their dawn-to-dusk routine of tending livestock and working in the fields drove Wright to exhaustion, but his Uncle James convinced him that he would get stronger the longer he worked and then he could endure anything. In his *An Autobiography* (1932), Wright described having "become a man" on the farm when he was entrusted with two horses to plow the fields. He wrote, "To be a man is to do a man's work." Wright loved being outdoors, and nature became his classroom. Living summers on the farm and winters with his parents in Madison continued until he was 16. Perhaps it was the farm work, coupled with a devotion to God and being the subject of adoration of the entire Lloyd-Jones clan, that provided young Wright with an enduring sense of purpose and confidence in his abilities. This assuredness appeared to others in later years as arrogance, but Wright was never disturbed by what other people thought of him.

During most of Frank's adolescence, the Wright family lived close to poverty. After years of earning a meager living by part-time preaching and teaching music, William Wright left his family. Frank was very sensitive to the shame that was attached to divorce in the late 1800s and personally felt the social stigma attached to his mother, who was labeled a "divorced woman." Neither parent ever remarried, and his mother always hoped that William Wright would return to his family, but Frank never saw his father again.

EDUCATION

In 1884, Wright enrolled at the University of Wisconsin. Because there was no school of architecture there, he enrolled in the School of

Engineering, where he also worked part-time as a draftsman. He was bored with his studies and felt that he was not learning to be a "real architect." Furthermore, he was concerned about the costs of his college education to his impoverished family. In late 1886, during his senior year, he left school before graduation to work in Chicago. He had to convince his disappointed mother that what his education lacked was "experience."

Despite his dissatisfaction with his studies, there was one dramatic event that he witnessed while in college that had a huge effect on him. On his way to classes one day, as he passed the State Capitol, an addition under construction collapsed in a huge cloud of dust, killing and injuring many of the workers. The terror of that scene haunted him throughout his career and contributed to the solidity of his buildings. For example, his Midway Gardens in Chicago, an open-air entertainment center built in 1913-14, was so durable and sturdy that when the city decided at the end of the 1920s to tear the building down, many contractors went bankrupt in the attempt.

FIRST JOBS

Wright's first job after leaving the University of Wisconsin was as a draftsman at $8 a week for the firm of J. L. Silsbee, which was building a church for his uncle, Chicago minister Jenkin Lloyd-Jones. A year later, in 1888, Wright designed his first completed structure, a house for his aunts in Spring Green, Wisconsin. He soon left Silsbee to work for $25 a week as a designer for Louis Sullivan, an established pioneer in the world of architecture and the architect who most influenced Wright. As Sullivan preferred to work on commercial structures, Wright assumed more responsibility for the building of residential houses, which became his trademark. By 1893, Wright was ready to establish his own architectural firm.

CAREER HIGHLIGHTS

The 1890s marked the beginning of Wright's "Prairie house" style of residential architecture, where the houses fit snugly into the landscapes for which they were designed; Wright called it "organic architecture." It was his intent to break away from the traditional box shape and to get in touch with nature, as his own words indicated: "A house, we like to believe, can be a noble consort to man and the trees." Wright was not only interested in creating a beautiful living space on the inside but was extremely involved with the harmonic blend of the exterior of the house with the land on which it was to be situated. These houses were abstract, full of geometric designs, with emphasis on vertical and horizontal lines. Large windows allow the interior of the house to appear to melt into the exterior. These early works became the first of what later was known as

Interior of Coonley House, built in 1908, furnished in 1910

the contemporary style. The steeply pitched roofline was flattened, often eliminating second stories or attics. There were no large basements in these houses, as Wright found them unnecessary to the aesthetics of the house. The Coonley House, built in 1908 in Riverside, Illinois, was considered by Wright to be his most successful residential design because it represented the epitome of his organic style.

During this period, Wright worked on non-residential buildings also, notably the Larkin Building in Buffalo, New York, and the Unity Temple Church in Oak Park, Illinois. In the Larkin building, completed in 1904, he used poured concrete for the first time in a nonresidential structure. This was the first office building in the United States designed to be fireproof, using metal-framed plate-glass doors and windows and all-metal office furniture. The building even had air-conditioning, almost unheard of in the early 1900s. Consistent with his philosophy that everyone should be able to enjoy and appreciate the beauty of architecture, he designed the central space for the office clerical staff with skylights five stories overhead to flood the workers with sunlight.

The Unity Temple Church, which was completed in 1906, bears Wright's revolutionary trademark of verticals organized into a concrete structure much resembling the Larkin Building. The design of this place of worship for the Universalists of Oak Park represented Wright's belief that God is wherever humanity congregates. So he designed a "temple" that would provide a safe shelter, with no external ornamentation such as steeples soaring into the sky. It was to be a simple meeting place in which God would be felt in the shared companionship of mortal humans.

MID-LIFE CHANGES

By the time he was 40, Wright felt that he had reached the pinnacle of his career as an architect. The preparation of a requested monograph on his work to be published in Germany provided him with a much-needed change of pace. He traveled to Europe in 1910, and when he returned in 1911, he built his famous Taliesin House (pronounced tal-lee-essen) on one of his favorite hills in the Wisconsin River valley. Made of materials native to the area, Taliesin (meaning "shining brow" in Welsh) was an estate that included several types of buildings—house, studio, school, and farm. The structures were blended into the landscape, uniting the land and the buildings, rather than just placing them on the land. Taliesin endured many changes over the years, including two devastating fires, before it was renovated with the financial assistance of Wright's friends and turned into a school for architects.

Between 1915 and 1922, Wright worked on the Imperial Hotel in Tokyo, Japan, and absorbed much Japanese culture in his frequent travels there. This hotel marked not only an architectural achievement but an engineering one as well. He designed the building to withstand an earthquake by pouring the foundation onto soft mud where it could "float" and by using concrete supports for the floors. The hotel remained undamaged even after the devastating Tokyo earthquake of 1923.

During this period, Wright also designed a series of houses in southern California that revealed the influence of Mayan and Southwestern American Indian architecture. Showing his innovative use of materials, he constructed these houses with precast concrete blocks threaded with metal reinforcements. During the late 1920s and early 1930s, Wright built few houses as the world fell into economic depression.

LATER YEARS

In late 1932 the Taliesin House in Wisconsin became a school, known as the Taliesin Fellowship, where Wright eventually provided training for hundreds of young architects. One of Wright's students idolized the architect to the extent that he convinced his wealthy businessman father to commission the architect to build a vacation house on a site overlooking a waterfall. The result was Fallingwater at Bear Run, Pennsylvania, completed in 1936. Fallingwater is one of the most famous homes ever built and perhaps the most beautiful of all the Wright houses. It is a marvel to view the structure suspended over the rushing waterfall.

It was at this time that Wright foresaw the need for a winter "campus" for his architects' workshops, leading him to design Taliesin West near Phoenix, Arizona. In this location, a desert camp was created of stone walls, redwood beams, and ceilings made only of canvas. In this warm, pleasant environment far from the harsh Wisconsin winters, Wright thought and talked about social institutions and the engineering of a truly democratic society. He felt that architecture had a role to play in this quest.

The concept of an attractive, distinctly American house affordable to middle-income families appealed to Wright. By the mid-1930s, he had begun building houses that would combine economy with functional design. He referred to these houses as "Usonian" to represent the democratic ideal. Dozens of these low-to-the-ground, winding, ranch-style houses were built. Unfortunately, their construction was too complicated and costly for a mid-price house builder. Although the concept later influenced the construction of affordable suburban housing, his designs at that time did not flourish.

Wright's enthusiasm for building renewed itself after the mid-1930s, and he began designing again at full speed. The more visible results of his later years were several buildings on the Florida Southern College campus in Lakeland, Florida, built from the late 1930s and unfinished when

Fallingwater, 1936, view from below

he died; the unique 15-story Johnson Wax Company research laboratory (1950) in Racine, Wisconsin; the Solomon R. Guggenheim Memorial Museum (1952-59) in New York City; and the Marin County Civic Center (1962) in San Raphael, California. The Guggenheim caused a sensation with its circular design and galleries linked by a spiral ramp instead of the traditional separate floors joined by stairs. Some Wright designs were completed after his death in Phoenix, Arizona, on April 9, 1959.

MARRIAGE AND FAMILY

Frank Lloyd Wright was married three times. In 1889, he married Catherine Lee Clark Tobin. They had six children before separating in 1910, although they were not legally divorced until 1923. Wright left his wife Catherine to sail to Europe with a client's wife, Mamah Cheney. Thereafter, Wright and Cheney established a home at Taliesin in Wisconsin. Tragically, while Wright was at work in Chicago one day in 1914, a dismissed Taliesin employee became crazed and murdered Cheney, her two children, and three Taliesin employees and then set the house on fire. (In 1925, the estate suffered a second fire.)

In 1923, immediately after his divorce from Catherine became final, Wright married Miriam Noel. A sculptor, Noel was addicted to drugs and emotionally unstable, and their marriage lasted only five years. His next marriage in 1928 was to Olgivanna Lazovich, a dancer from Montenegro (now a part of Yugoslavia), with whom he had had a daughter in 1925. It was with Lazovich that he founded his school for architects at Taliesin.

PHILOSOPHY AS AN ARCHITECT

Wright's philosophy of organic architecture required the harmony of all the elements—the interior and exterior design, the materials, and the landscape. For Wright, the unity of design was of paramount importance. He also strongly believed that architecture could play a role in a democratic society.

Wright felt passionate about the harmony of design, the pleasing arrangement of all the different parts. To help achieve this unity of interior and exterior, he began to create furniture appropriate for each individual house—he was disturbed when his clients moved their old furniture into his newly built designs. "Decoration," he wrote, "is intended to make use more charming and comfort more appropriate, or else a privilege has been abused." Wright also created dishes, pottery, and various adornments for the homes he designed. The structure's materials were also essential to the harmony he tried to create. He selected materials for his houses based on the design of the structure. As he wrote in his autobiography, "Appropriate designs for one material would not be appropriate at all for another material." Finally, the structure's design and materials were blended into the landscape of the site so all elements were harmonious.

While Wright was building his Usonian houses, he was passionate about the movement of people out of American cities due to the automobile and the creation of a less-centralized government. As a result, he designed what he considered to be an ideal environment, merging town and country to provide the inhabitants with a sense of community and private land. This development, known as Broadacre City, was never realized. The fascinating 12-foot-square model of this city is still a highlight of major exhibitions of his work.

Wright was productive both as an architect and as a writer. He is credited with designing more than 600 completed buildings and with writing 17 books. The legend of Frank Lloyd Wright is as impressive as his works. On the one hand, he was criticized for his incredible arrogance. He has been quoted as saying "Early in life, I had to choose between honest arrogance and hypocritical humility; I chose arrogance." But on the other hand, he was emotional, dedicated to his beliefs, and so full of life that people were drawn to him. He believed in the democratic ideals on which the United States was founded and often argued for them in his writings and lectures. Although he lived apart from the community of people who were the subject of his social engineering fantasies, his strong social consciousness kept alive his vision of bringing architecture to the masses.

LEGACY

Frank Lloyd Wright was an enigmatic, complex, and controversial figure. Yet few dispute that he was a genius, the greatest architect ever produced in America. His enduring appeal was explored in 1994 by Martin Filler, in a retrospective essay in *House Beautiful* magazine. "Why is Wright still so popular and what do his works mean today?" Filler wrote. "[Wright's designs] all bear the stamp of a stupendous personality the likes of which we will never see again. Wright is among the rare artists of the ages whose works will surely hold meaning for new generations, no matter how far removed they are from the maker's time and place. . . . [The] ability to inspire was Wright's gift to those around him, and even to those of us who look at his work today. Frank Lloyd Wright attempted nothing less than changing our way of seeing the world, and the degree to which he can still do it remains the truest measure of his genius."

Wright's legacy as an architect was also summed up by Filler. "Almost 35 years after his death, Frank Lloyd Wright remains America's best known and most beloved architect, and deservedly so. Unlike many other great artists who have passed into posthumous obscurity, Wright continues to speak to us through his work in ways that are deeply meaningful today. Respect for the environment, disdain for passing fashion, and an insistence that architecture encourage the wholeness of human experience are the major themes of Wright that put him ahead of his time.

"Although Wright designed a number of superb public buildings—such as Unity Temple in Oak Park, Illinois, the Johnson Wax headquarters in Racine, Wisconsin, and New York's Guggenheim Museum—he is above all remembered as the architect of some of America's most wonderful houses. With every passing decade, Wright's conception of the house as a sanctuary at once protective and open, comforting but challenging, rooted in its place and yet universal, seems more and more the epitome of mankind's intelligent response to nature."

MAJOR INFLUENCES

His family had an enormous influence on Wright, but his thought and style were also shaped by Socrates, Jesus, and William Shakespeare. American authors Ralph Waldo Emerson, Walt Whitman, and Henry David Thoreau were virtual heroes to Wright.

SELECTED WRITINGS

The Japanese Print, 1912
Experimenting with Human Lives, 1923
Modern Architecture, 1931
Two Lectures on Architecture, 1931
An Autobiography: Frank Lloyd Wright, 1932
The Disappearing City, 1932
Architecture and Modern Life, 1937 (with Baker Brownell)
An Organic Architecture, *1939*
Selected Writings on Architecture, 1941
When Democracy Builds, 1945
Genius and Mobocracy, 1949

HONORS AND AWARDS

Royal Gold Medal for Architecture (England): 1941
Gold Medal (American Institute of Architects): 1949
Italian Star of Solidarity: 1951
Gold Medal of the City of Florence: 1951
Gold Medal (American Academy and Institute of Arts and Letters): 1953

FURTHER READING

BOOKS

Boulton, Alexander O. *Frank Lloyd Wright: Architect*, 1993 (juvenile)
Contemporary Architects, 1994
Encyclopedia Americana, 1995
Encyclopedia Britannica, 1995
McDonough, Yona Zeldis. *Frank Lloyd Wright*, 1992 (juvenile)
Murphy, Wendy B. *Frank Lloyd Wright*, 1990 (juvenile)
Rubin, Susan Goldman. *Frank Lloyd Wright*, 1994 (juvenile)
Secrest, Meryle. *Frank Lloyd Wright: A Biography*, 1992
Thorne-Thomsen, Kathleen. *Frank Lloyd Wright for Kids*, 1994 (juvenile)
Twombly, Robert C. *Frank Lloyd Wright: An Interpretive Biography*, 1973
Who Was Who, Vol. III
World Book Encyclopedia, 1996
Wright, Frank Lloyd. *An Autobiography: Frank Lloyd Wright*, 1932

PERIODICALS

American Heritage, July/Aug. 1991, p.62
Architectural Digest, Mar. 1992, p.40
Current Biography Yearbook 1952; 1959 (obituary)
House Beautiful, June 1992, pp.18, 34 (and other articles); Jan. 1994, p.24;
    Mar. 1994, p.146
New York Times, Apr. 10, 1959, p.1; Apr. 13, 1959, p.31
New York Times Biographical Service, June 1992, p.734
New York Times Magazine, Feb. 13, 1994, p.48
New Yorker, Apr. 18, 1959, p.33
Smithsonian, Feb. 1994, p.54
Time, Apr. 20, 1959, p.80; Oct. 5, 1992, p.86

Photo and Illustration Credits

Ansel Adams: AP/Wide World. *Half Dome, Blowing Snow, Yosemite National Park*, c. 1955. Photograph by Ansel Adams. Copyright © 1995 by the Trustees of the Ansel Adams Publishing Rights Trust. All Rights Reserved.

Romare Bearden: Romare Howard Bearden Foundation, Inc. *Evening: 9:10 461 Lenox Avenue*, 1964. Courtesy Estate of Romare Bearden/ACA Galleries New York, Munich.

Margaret Bourke-White: AP/Wide World. *Buchenwald*, Margaret Bourke-White, LIFE Magazine; Copyright © Time, Inc.

Alexander Calder: AP/Wide World. *Hanging Spider*, 1940. Painted sheet metal and wire 49½ x 35½ in. (125.7 x 90.2 cm). Collection of Whitney Museum of American Art; Mrs. John B. Putnam Bequest. Photograph copyright © 1996: Whitney Museum of American Art. Artwork copyright Artists Rights Society. *Calderberry Bush*, 1932. Variation: *Object with Red Disks*. Painted steel rod, wire, wood and sheet aluminum. Dimensions variable, with base: 88½ x 33 x 47½ in. (224.8 x 83.8 x 120.7 cm.). Base: 24¼ x 24¼ x 24¼ (61.6 x 61.6 x 61.6 cm). Collection of Whitney Museum of American Art. Purchase, with funds from the Mrs. Percy Uris Purchase Fund. Photograph copyright © 1996: Whitney Museum of American Art. Artwork copyright Artists Rights Society.

Marc Chagall: AP/Wide World. *The Fiddler*. Copyright Artists Rights Society; Kunstsammlung Nordrhein-Westfalen, Duesseldorf, Germany. Courtesy Erich Lessing/Art Resource, NY.

Helen Frankenthaler: Helen Frankenthaler at Tyler Graphics, Ltd., 1993. Photo by Marabeth Cohen-Tyler. *Nature Abhors a Vacuum*, 1973. Acrylic on Canvas. 8' 7½' x 9' 4½". Private Collection. Courtesy of Andre Emmerich Gallery. Copyright © 1996 by Helen Frankenthaler.

Jasper Johns: AP/Wide World. *Target with Four Faces*, 1955. Encaustic and collage on canvas with plaster casts. 30" x 26". Photograph by Rudolph Burckhardt. Courtesy of Leo Castelli Gallery. Copyright © 1996 by VAGA, Inc.

Jacob Lawrence: Spike Mafford Photography. *Strength*, 1952. Courtesy of DC Moore Gallery.

Henry Moore: UPI/Bettmann. *Reclining Figure*, 1929. 84 cm. Brown Hornton Stone. Leeds City Art Gallery. Reproduced by permission of The Henry Moore Foundation. *The Family Group*, 1945/49. 152 cm. Bronze. Tate Gallery-London. Reproduced by permission of The Henry Moore Foundation.

Grandma Moses: AP/Wide World. The Bettmann Archive.

Louise Nevelson: UPI/Bettmann. *Dawn's Wedding Chapel II*, 1959. White painted wood. Including base: 115⅞ x 83½x10½ in. (294.3 x 212.1 x 26.7 cm). Collection of Whitney Museum of American Art. Purchase, with funds from the Howard and Jean Lipman Foundation, Inc. Photograph copyright © 1996: Whitney Museum of American Art.

Georgia O'Keeffe: AP/Wide World (Doris Bry; Courtesy of the Art Institute of Chicago). *Summer Days*, 1936. AP/Wide World. Copyright © 1996 by Artists Rights Society.

Gordon Parks: UPI/Bettmann. *Willie Causey Family*, 1956. Gordon Parks, LIFE Magazine. Copyright © 1956 Time Inc.

I.M. Pei: AP/Wide World. *John F. Kennedy Memorial Library*. Photograph copyright © 1996 by Nathaniel Lieberman. *Grand Louvre: Pyramid with Spraying Water Jets*, 1989. Photograph copyright © Stephane Couturier/ ARCHIPRESS.

Diego Rivera: Rivera finishing North Wall, 1932-33. Copyright © 1987 The Detroit Institute of Arts. *Detroit Industry*, North, Vaccination Panel. Photograph © 1996 The Detroit Institute of Arts, Founders Society Purchase, Edsel B. Ford Fund and Gift of Edsel B. Ford.

Norman Rockwell: AP/Wide World. *Freedom From Want*, 1943. Printed by permission of the Norman Rockwell Family Trust. Copyright © 1943. The Norman Rockwell Family Trust.

Andy Warhol: AP/Wide World. *The Twenty Marilyns*, 1962. Copyright © Artists Rights Society. Private Collection, Paris, France. Courtesy Giraudon/Art Resource, NY

Frank Lloyd Wright: Courtesy of The Frank Lloyd Wright Foundation. Coonley Residence, Interior, 1910. Courtesy of The Frank Lloyd Wright Foundation. Fallingwater, view from downstream, 1936. Margo Stipe. Courtesy of The Frank Lloyd Wright Foundation.

Name Index

Listed below are the names of all individuals profiled in *Biography Today*, followed by the date of the issue in which they appear.

General Index

This index includes subjects, occupations, organizations, and ethnic and minority origins that pertain to individuals profiled in *Biography Today*.

179

Jordan, Michael, 92/Jan;
  93/Update; 94/Update
Joyner-Kersee, Jackie, 92/Oct
Kerrigan, Nancy, 94/Apr
Lalas, Alexi, 94/Sep
Lemieux, Mario, 92/Jul;
  93/Update
Mantle, Mickey, 96/Jan
Marino, Dan, 93/Apr
Messier, Mark, 96/Apr
Miller, Shannon, 94/Sep
Montana, Joe, 95/Jan
Navratilova, Martina, 93/Jan;
  94/Update
Ndeti, Cosmas, 95/Sep
Olajuwon, Hakeem, 95/Sep
O'Neal, Shaquille, 93/Sep
Pippen, Scottie, 92/Oct
Rice, Jerry, 93/Apr
Rodman, Dennis, 96/Apr
Rose, Pete, 92/Jan
Rudolph, Wilma, 95/Apr
Ryan, Nolan, 92/Oct; 93/Update
Sanders, Barry, 95/Sep
Seles, Monica, 96/Jan
Smith, Emmitt, 94/Sep
Ward, Charlie, 94/Apr
Winfield, Dave, 93/Jan
Yamaguchi, Kristi, 92/Apr
Zmeskal, Kim, 94/Jan
Attorney General, U.S.
  Reno, Janet, 93/Sep
Australian
  Norman, Greg, 94/Jan
authors
  Angelou, Maya, 93/Apr
  Asimov, Isaac, 92/Jul
  Avi, 93/Jan
  Blume, Judy, 92/Jan
  Carle, Eric, 95/Author
  Carter, Jimmy, 95/Apr
  Childress, Alice, 95/Author
  Cormier, Robert, 95/Author
  Cleary, Beverly, 94/Apr

Cosby, Bill, 92/Jan
Dahl, Roald, 95/Author
Dove, Rita, 94/Jan
Duncan, Lois, 93/Sep
Filipovic, Zlata, 94/Sep
Grisham, John, 95/Author
Haley, Alex, 92/Apr
Hamilton, Virginia, 95/Author
Handford, Martin, 92/Jan
Herriot, James, 95/Author
Hinton, S.E., 95/Author
Iacocca, Lee A., 92/Jan
Kerr, M.E., 95/Author
King, Stephen, 95/Author
L'Engle, Madeleine, 92/Jan
Limbaugh, Rush, 95/Sep
Lovell, Jim, 96/Jan
Martin, Ann M., 92/Jan
McCully, Emily Arnold, 92/Jul;
  93/Update
Morrison, Toni, 94/Jan
Myers, Walter Dean, 93/Jan;
  94/Update
Naylor, Phyllis Reynolds,
  93/Apr
Nixon, Joan Lowery, 95/Author
Nixon, Richard, 94/Sep
Paulsen, Gary, 95/Author
Rylant, Cynthia, 95/Author
Scarry, Richard, 94/Sep
Seuss, Dr., 92/Jan
Speare, Elizabeth George, 95/Sep
Spinelli, Jerry, 93/Apr
Spock, Benjamin, 95/Sep
Steinem, Gloria, 92/Oct
Stine, R.L., 94/Apr
Taylor, Mildred D., 95/Author
Thomas, Lewis, 94/Apr
Van Allsburg, Chris, 92/Apr
Voigt, Cynthia, 92/Oct
Vonnegut, Kurt, Jr., 95/Author
White, E.B., 95/Author
Zindel, Paul, 95/Author

Kansas City Royals
Jackson, Bo, 92/Jan
Kenyan
Ndeti, Cosmas, 95/Sep
Ku Klux Klan
Duke, David, 92/Apr
Labor Party (Israel)
Rabin, Yitzhak, 92/Oct;
93/Update; 94/Update
Laker Girl
Abdul, Paula, 92/Jan
"Late Show with
David Letterman"
Letterman, David, 95/Jan
lawyers
Babbitt, Bruce, 94/Jan
Boutros-Ghali, Boutros, 93/Apr
Clinton, Hillary Rodham,
93/Apr
Grisham, John, 95/Author
Reno, Janet, 93/Sep
librarians
Avi, 93/Jan
Cleary, Beverly, 94/Apr
"Life Goes On"
Burke, Chris, 93/Sep
literacy, promotion of
Bush, Barbara, 92/Jan
Los Angeles Kings
Gretzky, Wayne, 92/Jan;
93/Update
Los Angeles Lakers
Johnson, Magic, 92/Apr
Los Angeles Raiders
Jackson, Bo, 92/Jan; 93/Update
Lou Gehrig's disease
see amyotrophic lateral sclerosis
Marine Corps
Anderson, Terry, 92/Apr
Baker, James, 92/Oct
"Melrose Place"
Locklear, Heather, 95/Jan
Mexican
Rivera, Diego, 96/Artist

Miami Dolphins
Marino, Dan, 93/Apr
Shula, Don, 96/Apr
Microsoft Corp.
Gates, Bill, 93/Apr
military service
England
Dahl, Roald, 95/Author
Moore, Henry, 96/Artist
France
Cousteau, Jacques, 93/Jan
Israel
Rabin, Yitzhak, 92/Oct
U.S.
Army
Ashe, Arthur, 93/Sep
Asimov, Isaac, 92/Jul
Bearden, Romare, 96/Artist
Carle, Eric, 95/Author
Dole, Bob, 96/Jan
Garcia, Jerry, 96/Jan
Gore, Al, 93/Jan
Ice-T, 93/Apr
Johns, Jasper, 96/Artist
Jones, James Earl, 95/Jan
Myers, Walter Dean, 93/Jan
Paulsen, Gary, 95/Author
Powell, Colin, 92/Jan;
93/Update
Scarry, Richard, 94/Sep
Schwarzkopf, H. Norman,
92/Jan
Seuss, Dr., 92/Jan
Thomas, Dave, 96/Apr
Vonnegut, Kurt, Jr.,
95/Author
Coast Guard
Haley, Alex, 92/Apr
Lawrence, Jacob, 96/Artist
Marine Corps
Anderson, Terry, 92/Apr
Baker, James, 92/Oct
Navy
Bush, George, 92/Jan

de Klerk, F.W., 94/Apr
Gorbachev, Mikhail, 92/Jan
Mandela, Nelson, 94/Update
McClintock, Barbara, 92/Oct
Menchu, Rigoberta, 93/Jan
Morrison, Toni, 94/Jan
Ochoa, Severo, 94/Jan
Pauling, Linus, 95/Jan
Oakland Athletics, batboy
Hammer, 92/Jan
obituaries
Adams, Ansel, 96/Artist
Anderson, Marian, 94/Jan
Ashe, Arthur, 93/Sep
Asimov, Isaac, 92/Jul
Bearden, Romare, 96/Artist
Bourke-White, Margaret,
96/Artist
Burger, Warren, 95/Sep
Calder, Alexander, 96/Artist
Candy, John, 94/Sep
Chagall, Marc, 96/Artist
Chavez, Cesar, 93/Sep
Childress, Alice, 95/Author
Cobain, Kurt, 94/Sep
Dahl, Roald, 95/Author
de Mille, Agnes, 95/Jan
Garcia, Jerry, 96/Jan
Gillespie, Dizzy, 93/Apr
Haley, Alex, 92/Apr
Hargreaves, Alison, 96/Jan
Herriot, James, 95/Author
Jordan, Barbara, 96/Apr
Mantle, Mickey, 96/Jan
Marshall, Thurgood, 93/Update
Masih, Iqbal, 96/Jan
McClintock, Barbara, 92/Oct
Moore, Henry, 96/Artist
Moses, Grandma, 96/Artist
Nevelson, Louise, 96/Artist
Nixon, Richard, 94/Sep
Nureyev, Rudolf, 93/Apr
Ochoa, Severo, 94/Jan

O'Keeffe, Georgia, 96/Artist
Pauling, Linus, 95/Jan
Phoenix, River, 94/Apr
Rivera, Diego, 96/Artist
Rockwell, Norman, 96/Artist
Rudolph, Wilma, 95/Apr
Scarry, Richard, 94/Sep
Selena, 96/Jan
Seuss, Dr., 92/Jan
Speare, Elizabeth George, 95/Sep
Thomas, Lewis, 94/Apr
Warhol, Andy, 96/Artist
White, E.B., 95/Author
Wright, Frank Lloyd, 96/Artist
Zamora, Pedro, 95/Apr
oil executive
Bush, George, 92/Jan
Olympics
Baiul, Oksana, 95/Apr
Bird, Larry, 92/Jan
Blair, Bonnie, 94/Apr
Evans, Janet, 95/Jan
Ewing, Patrick, 95/Jan
Harding, Tonya, 94/Sep
Jansen, Dan, 94/Apr
Joyner-Kersee, Jackie, 92/Oct
Kerrigan, Nancy, 94/Apr
Miller, Shannon, 94/Sep
Rudolph, Wilma, 95/Apr
Yamaguchi, Kristi, 92/Apr
Zmeskal, Kim, 94/Jan
opera
Anderson, Marian, 94/Jan
Battle, Kathleen, 93/Jan
Domingo, Placido, 95/Sep
"Oprah Winfrey Show, The"
Winfrey, Oprah, 92/Apr
Orlando Magic
O'Neal, Shaquille, 93/Sep
painters
Chagall, Marc, 96/Artist
Frankenthaler, Helen, 96/Artist
Johns, Jasper, 96/Artist

Places of Birth Index

The following index lists the places of birth for the individuals profiled in *Biography Today*. Places of birth are entered under state, province, and/or country.

203

Birthday Index

July, continued
24 Krone, Julie (1963)
28 Davis, Jim (1945)
29 Burns, Ken (1953)
   Dole, Elizabeth Hanford (1936)
   Jennings, Peter (1938)
   Morris, Wanya (1973)
30 Hill, Anita (1956)
   Moore, Henry (1898)

August
1 Garcia, Jerry (1942)
3 Roper, Dee Dee
5 Ewing, Patrick (1962)
6 Warhol, Andy (1928?)
7 Duchovny, David (1960)
9 Houston, Whitney (1963)
11 Haley, Alex (1921)
   Hogan, Hulk (1953)
12 Martin, Ann M. (1955)
   Myers, Walter Dean (1937)
13 Battle, Kathleen (1948)
   Castro, Fidel (1927)
14 Berry, Halle (1967?)
   Johnson, Magic (1959)
   Larson, Gary (1950)
15 Ellerbee, Linda (1944)
19 Clinton, Bill (1946)
20 Chung, Connie (1946)
22 Schwarzkopf, H. Norman (1934)
23 Novello, Antonia (1944)
   Phoenix, River (1970)
24 Arafat, Yasir (1929)
26 Burke, Christopher (1965)
   Culkin, Macaulay (1980)
28 Dove, Rita (1952)
   Evans, Janet (1971)
   Priestley, Jason (1969)
31 Perlman, Itzhak (1945)

September
1 Estefan, Gloria (1958)
2 Bearden, Romare (1912?)
   Galeczka, Chris (1981)

5 Guisewite, Cathy (1950)
7 Lawrence, Jacob (1917)
   Moses, Grandma (1860)
8 Thomas, Jonathan Taylor (1982)
13 Taylor, Mildred D. (1943)
15 Marino, Dan (1961)
16 Dahl, Roald (1916)
17 Burger, Warren (1907)
18 de Mille, Agnes (1905)
   Fields, Debbi (1956)
21 Fielder, Cecil (1963)
   King, Stephen (1947)
23 Nevelson, Louise (1899)
24 Ochoa, Severo (1905)
25 Locklear, Heather (1961)
   Lopez, Charlotte (1976)
   Pippen, Scottie (1965)
   Smith, Will (1968)
   Walters, Barbara (1931)
26 Stockman, Shawn (1972)
27 Handford, Martin (1956)

October
1 Carter, Jimmy (1924)
3 Herriot, James (1916)
   Winfield, Dave (1951)
5 Lemieux, Mario (1965)
7 Ma, Yo-Yo (1955)
8 Jackson, Jesse (1941)
   Stine, R.L. (1943)
11 Perry, Luke (1964?)
   Young, Steve (1961)
12 Childress, Alice (1920?)
   Ward, Charlie (1970)
13 Kerrigan, Nancy (1969)
   Rice, Jerry (1962)
15 Iacocca, Lee A. (1924)
17 Jemison, Mae (1956)
18 Marsalis, Wynton (1961)
   Navratilova, Martina (1956)
20 Mantle, Mickey (1931)
21 Gillespie, Dizzy (1956)
26 Clinton, Hillary Rodham (1947)
27 Anderson, Terry (1947)

People to Appear in Future Issues

Actors
Trini Alvarado
Gillian Anderson
Richard Dean
  Anderson
Dan Aykroyd
Tyra Banks
Drew Barrymore
Zachary Ty Bryan
Levar Burton
Cher
Kevin Costner
Courtney Cox
Tom Cruise
Jamie Lee Curtis
Patti D'Arbanville-
  Quinn
Geena Davis
Ozzie Davis
Ruby Dee
Michael De Lorenzo
Matt Dillon
Michael Douglas
Larry Fishburne
Harrison Ford
Jody Foster
Morgan Freeman
Richard Gere
Tracey Gold
Graham Greene
Mark Harmon
Michael Keaton
Val Kilmer
Angela Lansbury
Joey Lawrence
Martin Lawrence
Christopher Lloyd
Heather Locklear
Kellie Martin
Marlee Matlin
Bette Midler
Alyssa Milano
Demi Moore
Rick Moranis
Tamera Mowry
Tia Mowry
Kate Mulgrew
Eddie Murphy
Liam Neeson
Leonard Nimoy
Rosie O'Donnell
Sean Penn
Phylicia Rashad
Keanu Reeves
Jason James Richter
Julia Roberts
Bob Saget
Arnold
  Schwarzenegger
Alicia Silverstone
Christian Slater

Taran Noah Smith
Jimmy Smits
Wesley Snipes
Sylvester Stallone
John Travolta
Mario Van Peebles
Damon Wayans
Bruce Willis
B.D. Wong
Malik Yoba

Artists
Mitsumasa Anno
Graeme Base
Maya Ying Lin
Yoko Ono

Astronauts
Neil Armstrong

Authors
Jean M. Auel
Lynn Banks
Gwendolyn Brooks
John Christopher
Arthur C. Clarke
John Colville
Paula Danziger
Paula Fox
Patricia Reilly Gibb
Jamie Gilson
Rosa Guy
Nat Hentoff
Norma Klein
E.L. Konigsburg
Lois Lowry
David Macaulay
Stephen Manes
Norma Fox Mazer
Anne McCaffrey
Gloria D. Miklowitz
Marsha Norman
Robert O'Brien
Francine Pascal
Christopher Pike
Daniel Pinkwater
Ann Rice
Louis Sachar
Carl Sagan
J.D. Salinger
John Saul
Maurice Sendak
Shel Silverstein
Amy Tan
Alice Walker
Jane Yolen
Roger Zelazny

Business
Minoru Arakawa
Michael Eisner

David Geffen
Wayne Huizenga
Donna Karan
Phil Knight
Estee Lauder
Sheri Poe
Anita Roddick
Donald Trump
Ted Turner
Lillian Vernon

Cartoonists
Lynda Barry
Roz Chast
Greg Evans
Nicole Hollander
Charles Schulz
Art Spiegelman
Garry Trudeau

Comedians
Billy Crystal
Steve Martin
Eddie Murphy
Bill Murray

Dancers
Debbie Allen
Mikhail
  Baryshnikov
Gregory Hines
Twyla Tharp
Tommy Tune

Directors/
  Producers
Woody Allen
Steven Bocho
Tim Burton
Francis Ford
  Coppola
Ron Howard
John Hughes
George Lucas
Penny Marshall
Leonard Nimoy
Rob Reiner
John Singleton
Quentin Tarantino

Environmentalists/
  Animal Rights
Marjory Stoneman
  Douglas
Kathryn Fuller
Lois Gibbs
Wangari Maathai
Linda Maraniss
Ingrid Newkirk
Pat Potter

Journalists
Tom Brokaw
John Hockenberry
Ted Koppel
Jim Lehrer
Dan Rather
Nina Totenberg
Mike Wallace
Bob Woodward

Musicians
Ace of Base
Babyface
Basia
George Benson
Bjork
Clint Black
Ruben Blades
Mary J. Blige
Bono
Edie Brickell
James Brown
Ray Charles
Chayanne
Natalie Cole
Coolio
Cowboy Junkies
Sheryl Crow
Billy Ray Cyrus
Melissa Etheridge
Aretha Franklin
Green Day
Guns N' Roses
P.J. Harvey
Hootie & the
  Blowfish
India
Janet Jackson
Michael Jackson
Winona Judd
R. Kelly
Anthony Kiedis
Lenny Kravitz
Kris Kross
James Levine
LL Cool J
Andrew Lloyd
  Webber
Courtney Love
Lyle Lovett
MC Lyte
Madonna
Barbara Mandrell
Branford Marsalis
Paul McCartney
Midori
Alanis Morissette
Morrissey
N.W.A.
Jesseye Norman
Sinead O'Connor

211

Luciano Pavoratti
Pearl Jam
Teddy Pendergrass
David Pirner
Prince
Public Enemy
Raffi
Bonnie Raitt
Red Hot Chili
  Peppers
Lou Reed
L.A. Reid
R.E.M.
Trent Reznor
Kenny Rogers
Axl Rose
Run-D.M.C.
Paul Simon
Smashing Pumpkins
Sting
Michael Stipe
Pam Tillis
TLC
Randy Travis
Terence Trent
  d'Arby
Travis Tritt
U2
Eddie Vedder
Stevie Wonder
Trisha Yearwood
Dwight Yoakum
Neil Young

Politics/World
  Leaders
Madeleine Albright
Harry A. Blackmun
Jesse Brown
Ronald Brown
Pat Buchanan
Mangosuthu
  Buthelezi
Violeta Barrios de
  Chamorro

Shirley Chisolm
Jean Chretien
Warren Christopher
Edith Cresson
Mario Cuomo
Dalai Lama
Mike Espy
Alan Greenspan
Vaclav Havel
Jack Kemp
Bob Kerrey
Kim Il-Sung
Coretta Scott King
John Major
Imelda Marcos
Slobodan Milosevic
Mother Theresa
Ralph Nader
Manuel Noriega
Hazel O'Leary
Leon Panetta
Federico Pena
Simon Peres
Robert Reich
Ann Richards
Richard Riley
Phyllis Schlafly
Pat Schroeder
Donna Shalala
Desmond Tutu
Lech Walesa
Eli Weisel
Vladimir
  Zhirinovsky

Royalty
Charles, Prince of
  Wales
Duchess of York
  (Sarah Ferguson)
Queen Noor

Scientists
Sallie Baliunas
Avis Cohen

Donna Cox
Jane Goodall
Stephen Jay Gould
Mimi Koehl
Deborah Letourneau
Philippa Marrack
Helen Quinn
Carl Sagan
Barbara Smuts
Flossie Wong-Staal
Aslihan Yener
Adrienne Zihlman

Sports
Jim Abbott
Muhammad Ali
Michael Andretti
Boris Becker
Barry Bonds
Bobby Bonilla
Jose Canseco
Jennifer Capriati
Michael Chang
Roger Clemens
Randall
  Cunningham
Eric Davis
Clyde Drexler
John Elway
Chris Evert
George Foreman
Zina Garrison
Florence Griffith-
  Joyner
Anfernee Hardaway
Rickey Henderson
Evander Holyfield
Brett Hull
Raghib Ismail
Jim Kelly
Petr Klima
Carl Lewis
Willy Mays
Paul Molitor
Jack Nicklaus

Joe Paterno
Kirby Puckett
Pat Riley
Mark Rippien
David Robinson
Deion Sanders
Daryl Strawberry
Danny Sullivan
Vinnie Testaverde
Isiah Thomas
Mike Tyson
Steve Yzerman

Television
  Personalities
Andre Brown (Dr.
  Dre)
Katie Couric
Phil Donahue
Kathie Lee Gifford
Ed Gordon
Bryant Gumbel
Arsenio Hall
Ricki Lake
Joan Lunden
Dennis Miller
Diane Sawyer
Tabitha Soren
Alison Stewart
Jon Stewart
Vanna White
Montel Williams
Paul Zaloom

Other
James Brady
Johnnetta Cole
David Copperfield
Jaimie Escalante
Jack Kevorkian
Wendy Kopp
Sister Irene Kraus
Jeanne White